D0346917

Wendy Hobson has spent a career in creative publishing, both as author and commissioning editor. She has worked for a range of top international publishers and with chefs as respected as Ken Hom, Gary Rhodes and Mary Berry. With cookery a particular speciality, her published books include *Everyday Cooking for One*, *Home Baking* series, *Classic 1000 Recipes*, *Classic 1000 Cake & Bake Recipes* as well as *Simply Feng Shui* and *Silver Surfers' Colour Guide to Word Processing*. Wendy has edited thousands of books, from Daniel Galmiche's *Revolutionary French Cooking* to the best-selling UK travel guide *Brit Guide Orlando*.

Also available from Constable & Robinson

Everyday Cooking For One

Everyday Thai Cooking

How To Cook Your Favourite Takeaways At Home

Healthy Eating for Life

The No-Waste Meal Planner

Making the Most of Your Food Processor

Making the Most of Your Pressure Cooker

MEALS in a MUG

100 delicious recipes ready to eat in minutes

WENDY HOBSON

RIGHT
WAY

Constable & Robinson Ltd
55–56 Russell Square
London WC1B 4HP
www.constablerobinson.com

First published in the UK by Right Way,
an imprint of Constable & Robinson Ltd, 2014

Text copyright © Wendy Hobson 2014
Illustrations © Firecatcher Creative, www.firecatcher.co.uk

The right of Wendy Hobson to be identified as the author of this work has been
asserted by her in accordance with the Copyright, Designs & Patents Act 1988.

All rights reserved. This book is sold subject to the condition that it shall not, by way
of trade or otherwise, be lent, re-sold, hired out or otherwise circulated in any form of
binding or cover other than that in which it is published and without a similar
condition including this condition being imposed on the subsequent purchaser.

A copy of the British Library Cataloguing in Publication Data
is available from the British Library

ISBN: 978-0-7160-2392-0 (paperback)
ISBN: 978-0-7160-2393-7 (ebook)

1 3 5 7 9 10 8 6 4 2

Printed and bound in the EU

Contents

Introduction

While a mug and a microwave may not conjure up visions of *cordon bleu* restaurants, the reality is that there are times when we all need something quick and easy to eat, just for one. How often do you come in late from work and just fancy something hot and nutritious but can't be bothered to go to the trouble of cooking a meal? If you have teenage children coming home from school, there's no way they can wait until dinner to have something to eat. Or perhaps your family has days when your schedules just don't coincide and someone ends up hungry and in a rush to be somewhere else.

If you work in an office, you may have wondered why they bother to put a microwave in the kitchen when most people resort to their box of sandwiches, or complain how much they have to pay to buy a sandwich from the shop down the road. Well, now you know! That under-used microwave is just waiting for you to ditch those dull sandwiches and conjure up a neat little meal all for yourself. And how could we forget the cash incentive? We have all been feeling the pinch of late, so saving your sandwich money will soon add up.

So whether you are a busy mum trying to juggle family schedules, a student strapped for cash, an office worker keen to consign that boring lunch box to the bin, a teenager coming home hungry from school, a shift worker out of sync with the family's mealtimes, a young or old person living alone and not always keen to go to the trouble of cooking a meal … read on.

All these recipes are quick, simple to follow and make a meal in a mug. (Well, sometimes you'll find a big cappuccino cup works better, but I think that's fair.)

This may not be a sustainable diet for every day, but there are days when everyone will find these recipes not only useful and tasty but also surprisingly good. And it must be better to cook from scratch so you know exactly what you are eating than to constantly reach for the dehydrated packet or the cheap ready meal. Plus they do include fresh ingredients and there are some interesting salads too.

You will find that for some recipes – notably those made with pasta and rice – there is a slight problem to overcome. It is much easier to cook the first stage in a larger bowl because there is not enough room in a mug for the ingredients to boil and rise up: they just overflow and make a mess. The recipes all take this into account, but do be wary of this when you are trying out your own recipes.

So dip in and try a few recipes and you'll soon see that, with a little imagination, you can, indeed, make a tasty, fun and enjoyable meal … in a mug …. in a microwave.

P.S.

And did I mention that in just a few minutes you can rustle up a little cake or dessert to satisfy an unexpected guest, give a child a special treat or feed that sweet tooth? Or that the imaginative dinner-party hostess can serve a quirky, individual starter or dessert to impress the new neighbours?

Do I really only need a mug?

A mug, a microwave and a spoon are really all you need for most of the recipes in this book. Add a knife and fork and a small whisk and you can expand your repertoire still more. Some recipes seem to work better – or are just easier to eat – if you make them in a wider mug or a cappuccino cup, but that's simply a matter of choice. It sounds obvious, but don't forget to choose a mug or cup that is suitable for the microwave – so that means no precious china or mugs with gold decorations. I used a 400 ml (14 fl oz) mug or an outsize cup for most recipes, which is what I call a 'large mug'. If your mug is a little larger than a standard mug, and a little wider at the top, it makes it easier to mix ingredients and is generally more convenient to use.

For some recipes – mainly those cooking pasta or rice – it is easier (but not essential) to use a microwave-safe bowl large enough for the liquid to bubble up when cooking, but I'll explain why when we start cooking rice dishes.

There is no weighing involved in the recipes, so all you need to prepare your ingredients are the usual things you have to hand in the kitchen – knife, whisk, spoons, sharp knife and chopping board. If you have a set of measuring spoons, then you can measure more accurately, but ordinary spoons will do. I also use a set of US cup measures to make things more convenient. If you don't have cup measures, select an ordinary cup that takes 250 ml (8 fl oz) and use that instead.

Everything in this handy book is designed for speed and convenience, so you should find you can make yourself a delicious meal ... in a mug ... in a microwave ... in minutes.

What to keep in the cupboard

Some people – and I confess to being one of them – always have a cupboard full of basic stocks so they don't have to go to the shops with a plan for every meal. Others prefer to shop only when they need something. For these recipes, a few store-cupboard items will prove particularly useful as they will make it possible for you to rustle up a simple but tasty mug-meal at a moment's notice.

With everyday meals and snacks like these that use such small quantities, you don't want to have to go out shopping every time you need a bite to eat – for a start, it makes a nonsense of the whole idea of 'quick and easy'. And you can't afford to use little bits of all kinds of ingredients and waste the rest. So a little advance planning is pretty much essential so that you can take full advantage of the recipes. Here are a few ideas for useful ingredients to keep in your cupboard.

- **Buy some frozen free-flow vegetables** You can take out a spoonful as and when you need them and use them straight from frozen. Diced onions, sweetcorn and peas are particularly handy.
- **Try free-flow frozen minced meat or meatballs** Frozen mince – beef, lamb, pork or turkey – that can be used straight from the freezer are as useful as frozen vegetables, as well as those little meatballs in the egg-box-style packs. If you do buy a pack of ordinary fresh mince, parcel it up in small quantities before freezing.
- **Choose goujons** Chicken or turkey goujons come ready-made in convenient, small portions.
- **A seafood diet** Prawns and other seafood are just made for quick and easy cooking in small quantities and store well in the freezer.
- **Take the easy way out** Jars of ready-chopped garlic and chilli are great when you are using small quantities and you can also buy more unusual items like lemongrass.
- **Go for jellied stock pots** These are easy to store – in the fridge for a couple of days once opened – and you can just add a small spoonful here and there for extra flavour.

- **Handy packets and cans** Canned tomatoes, tuna, chickpeas, sweetcorn and other vegetables are all useful, plus a packet of couscous and some noodles, and perhaps some instant mash.
- **Sprinkle with some dried fruit** A few sultanas, perhaps some figs or apricots, can brighten up lots of dishes – sweet or savoury. Keep only one or two of these things at a time in stock so they don't go out of date before you can use them.
- **Spice it up** Keep some black peppercorns in a grinder and a little sea salt, if you use it, although keep it to a minimum as it can overpower small portions. Something spicy – such as chilli or cayenne – will liven up all kinds of dishes. Mixed spice is a good all-purpose spice for cakes and bakes, although you may prefer cinnamon or nutmeg.
- **What about your windowsill?** Ideally, have a pot or two of herbs growing fresh on your windowsill.
- **Cake basics** Flour, baking powder, sugar, butter and eggs are your basic cake ingredients.

It sounds obvious, but don't buy things you know you'll never need – however useful someone else finds them. And if you only use something in very small quantities or very occasionally, don't be tempted to buy the larger size, even though it may be cheaper. You'll only find cans, jars or packets with embarrassing 'use by' dates next time you clear out the pantry.

And don't forget to keep a few salad items in the chiller drawer of your fridge and some fresh fruit to make sure you keep a healthy balance in your diet.

Tips on microwaving in a mug

The recipes are so easy that you don't need too many instructions. Just glance through these common-sense principles before you start.

- **Portions** The finished dish will not necessarily fill the mug but it will provide one portion. This constitutes a fairly generous portion in the case of the cakes and desserts, so you may find there's enough to share if you turn the food out of the mug.
- **700 watts** The recipes are all cooked on High, so I haven't specified a setting for each one. They were tested in a standard 700-watt microwave.
- **400 ml mug** A large, wide mug or a cappuccino cup are the easiest to use, about 400 ml (14 fl oz) capacity.
- **Rice, pasta and noodles** Use a bowl for rice and pasta to avoid the liquid boiling over, or follow the method for cooking in short bursts and topping up with boiling water, in which case you will need to watch that the liquid does not overflow. Make sure the ingredients are just tender before moving on!
- **Measurements** There's no weighing, just level spoonfuls or cups. Use a 250 ml (8 fl oz) cup measure, or just an ordinary teacup or something of a similar volume.
- **Stirring** Stir at regular intervals as suggested in the recipes. Sometimes it is easier to make sure all the ingredients are mixed in if you use a knife, which can get into the corners of the mug, rather than a spoon.
- **Softening butter** If you use softened butter, you'll find it easier to mix. If you have forgotten to take it out of the fridge in time, pop it in the microwave for 10–15 seconds.
- **Timings** Times are approximate as they will depend on your microwave and the size and shape of your mug. Always use the shortest time, then return the food to the microwave if it is not ready and cook in short bursts. You'll soon get used to your microwave and whether you need to increase or decrease the

recommended cooking times. Almost every recipe goes from cupboard to table in less than 10 minutes, with rice and pasta taking just a few minutes longer.

- **Resting times** Remember that the food will continue to cook after it comes out of the microwave, so allow it a short resting time before you eat.
- **Too hot to handle** Because it is still cooking, and is also in a confined mug, the food will get very hot – especially if it has a high sugar and fat content – so do be careful when removing it from the microwave and when you start to eat.
- **Seasoning** Only season very lightly otherwise you may spoil your dish. You can always add more when you start to eat.
- **Garnish** Food does not brown in a microwave, so a lightly coloured sauce or fresh herb garnish will improve the appearance.
- **Using traditional cooking methods** You can always combine cooking in the microwave with cooking on the hob or in the oven. You may want to tip some dishes on to a flameproof plate and flash them under a hot grill before serving.
- **Using leftovers** Because the quantities are small, the recipes are ideally suited to using up leftovers, so you can use items such as cooked meat or vegetables. Add them towards the end of the cooking time and heat through thoroughly.
- **Flexibility** I have tried to present as wide a variety of recipes as possible – some very simple and others with more ingredients or several stages in the method. Where there are quite a few ingredients, those putting together a last-minute meal may well not have everything available, but that doesn't matter. Improvise: substitute with what you do have, leave things out, make the recipe your own. There is no 'right' way to make any of these dishes – if you like it, that's right enough.

Meals on a budget

We all know we are supposed to eat five portions a day of healthy fruit and vegetables and plan our meals. All that is fine in theory, but the practice can often be a bit more random. If you are on a tight budget – especially if you are new to shopping and cooking for yourself – here are a few money-saving tips followed by some ideas on what to do when the cupboard really is bare.

BUDGET SURVIVAL TIPS
- Corner shops are wonderful but they are more expensive, so use them sparingly.
- Think about what you need before you go shopping. Write a list and stick to it.
- Try not to go shopping when you are hungry.
- Head straight for the items you want, especially if you only need a few, then to the checkout. Avoid browsing up and down the aisles – you are bound to pick up extras.
- Look for own-brand items instead of high-end brands.
- Buy items on special offer, but beware of BOGOF deals unless you are going to use up the food.
- Larger sizes are usually cheaper but only if you don't waste half of the produce. Can you share with a friend?
- Avoid the unusual, the exotic and the imported.
- Make sure you include something filling in your shopping, like potatoes, rice, bread or noodles.
- Root vegetables are great value, healthy and versatile.
- Buy some flour and yeast and make your own bread. (In a mug? Of course! You'll find a soda bread roll on page 17.)
- The more packaging and processing in the product, the more you will be paying for it.

Emergency meal planner

On those days when you are down to what you can identify at the bottom of the fridge – a forlorn can of something you can't remember buying and your last coin for the supermarket trolley – there's nothing for it but to improvise. Here are a few ideas that should convince you that all is not lost. Just add a little imagination.

YOUR INGREDIENTS
- Put everything you have on the work surface.
- Pick the item that will be the main ingredient. Worst-case scenario, this has to be what you have the most of. This could be meat, poultry or fish; vegetables or fruit; or perhaps a ready-made soup or meal.
- Now choose anything you have to fill you up – bread, rice, noodles, couscous.
- If you are lucky, you may have some supporting ingredients – anything that you think could go with your main item.
- Finally, look at what you have to brighten up or flavour your meal – spices, herbs, oil, a stock cube or a bottle of tomato sauce.

Once you've reached this point, your imagination should kick in and you will see that the situation is not as hopeless as you might have thought. Let's look at a few examples to give you some more ideas. This assumes you are cooking in a microwave but you could cook them on the hob instead. They'd all benefit from a little sprinkling of salt and pepper.

FISH 'N' DIPS
You have A day-old slice of bread, a leftover fish finger, some olive oil and mayonnaise, and a sachet of tomato ketchup.
What you can do with it Cut the bread into fingers and quarter the fish finger into 4 chunks or strips. Put a little oil on a plate, toss the bread and fish in it until coated, then microwave for 2 minutes until

heated through. Mix together equal quantities of mayonnaise and tomato ketchup to make a dip for the hot, crispy croûtons and fish.

Speedy carbonara
You have A handful of spaghetti or noodles, a clove of garlic, slice of ham and the tail end of a pot of cream. If you have a knob of butter, that's a bonus.
What you can do with it Cook the spaghetti in a bowl of water for about 8 minutes until just tender. Drain well. Chop the garlic and put it in a large mug with the butter, if you have it, or with a drop of water, and microwave for 1 minute. Chop the ham and drop it into the cream pot, then scrape it all into the mug with the butter and garlic and add the spaghetti. Stir everything together and microwave for 1–2 minutes to heat through.

Chicken soup with Parmesan croûte
You have A dull-looking packet of chicken soup, a spring onion, a hard lump of Parmesan cheese and a slice of yesterday's garlic bread.
What you can do with it Make up the chicken soup with water in a large mug or bowl and microwave for 2 minutes. Trim and chop the spring onion and add it to the soup, then continue to microwave for 4 minutes, stirring occasionally. Do this in 40-second bursts if you are using a mug. Grate the Parmesan finely and sprinkle on top of the bread, then brown under a hot grill. When the soup is ready, float the bread on top. Leave to stand for a couple of minutes to allow the soup to soak into the bread.

Sausage and potato surprise
You have A potato, an onion, a little stock, a sausage and an egg.
What you can do with it Peel and grate the potato and onion and mix together, then spoon loosely into a large mug. Pour in $1/2$ cup of stock and microwave for 5 minutes, in short bursts if necessary, until tender. Drain off any excess stock. Cut the sausage into chunks and put in a separate mug, then microwave for about 4 minutes until cooked. Gently press the potato and onion down over the sausages to

give a flat surface, then break the egg on top, pierce the yolk with a cocktail stick and microwave for 2 minutes until cooked.

MEDITERRANEAN SALAD

You have The end of a packet of couscous, half a pepper, a slightly soft apple and a few olives.

What you can do with it Put the couscous in a large mug and just cover with boiling water. Stir occasionally until the water has been absorbed and the couscous is soft; drain off any excess. Meanwhile, trim and chop the pepper, apple and olives. Stir them into the couscous and serve.

And if all else fails, take that final £1 and see how many fresh and nutritious vegetables you can get from the supermarket.

10

Breakfasts and brunch

We are constantly reminded that breakfast is the most important meal of the day as it should provide us with the slow-release energy we need to get us going – and keep us going until lunchtime. The first thing that springs to mind is porridge, which has long been a breakfast favourite and is quick and easy to make in the microwave. As it's such a healthy option, I have included a traditional and a modern version for you to enjoy. But that's not all. Delicious granola, hot cereal dishes and tasty egg-and-bacon feasts that can double up for brunch are all included, so there's no excuse to skip breakfast.

APRICOT PORRIDGE

Simply leave out the fruit and spice to make a traditional porridge. You can substitute other fruits for the apricots if you prefer: sultanas, chopped figs, chopped dates or chopped prunes are all good options.

1/4 cup rolled oats
1/2 cup milk, plus extra for serving
a tiny pinch of salt
a pinch of mixed spice
1 tbsp chopped ready-to-eat dried apricots
a drizzle of maple syrup or clear honey

---

1. Put the oats, milk, salt and mixed spice in a large mug and microwave for 2 minutes.
2. Stir well, then microwave for a further 1 minute.
3. Stir in the apricots and microwave for a further 30 seconds.
4. Stir well, then leave to stand for 2 minutes.
5. Serve with a little more milk and a drizzle of maple syrup or honey.

HOT CRANBERRY
AND ALMOND MUESLI

Use whatever you have in the cupboard to make different versions of this breakfast. Try using sultanas instead of cranberries; different nuts or seeds; syrup or agave nectar instead of honey. Or, after cooking, add half an apple, peeled, cored and chopped, or one-third of a banana, chopped.

8 tbsp rolled oats
2 tbsp dried cranberries
2 tbsp flaked almonds
1 tbsp ground almonds
1 tbsp flax seeds
1 tbsp sunflower seeds
a pinch of freshly grated nutmeg
1 egg
1 tsp clear honey
about ½ cup milk
1 tbsp plain yogurt

1. Put all the ingredients except the yogurt in a large mug and mix together well. Microwave for 2 minutes.
2. Stir again, then microwave for a further 2 minutes until soft and well blended.
3. Stir well, then top with a spoonful of yogurt.

GRANOLA

Make sure you stir the ingredients so that the honey, oil and maple syrup are distributed through the mixture.

$^3/_4$ cup rolled oats
3 tbsp dried cranberries
2 tbsp flaked almonds
2 tbsp desiccated coconut
1 tsp sunflower seeds
$^1/_2$ tsp sesame seeds
1 tbsp maple syrup
1 tsp sunflower oil
1 tsp clear honey
a few drops of vanilla extract
milk, to serve

---

1. Put all the ingredients except the milk in a large mug and mix together well. Microwave for 1 minute.
2. Stir well, then microwave for 30 seconds.
3. Stir again, then microwave for a further 30 seconds until all the ingredients are hot.
4. Leave to stand for 1 minute.
5. Serve warm or cold with a little milk.

QUICK MINI CROISSANTS

Since the name denotes the shape, I have tried to keep these six neat little croissants as close as possible to the original, although, of course, they won't brown in the microwave.

---

10 x 2.5 cm (4 x 1 in) piece of puff pastry
(taken from a block of ready-made pastry)
a little flour, for dusting
4 tbsp butter, softened
1 tbsp apricot jam, sieved
marmalade sauce, to serve

Marmalade sauce
$1/4$ cup orange juice
$1/3$ cup dark soft brown sugar
2 cloves
$3/4$ tsp cornflour
2 tbsp butter

---

1. Roll out the pastry on a lightly floured surface to a rectangle of about 24 x 12 cm (10 x 5 in); it will be quite thin. Cut into about 6 tall, thin triangles, re-rolling the trimmings to use all the pastry.
2. Spread the pastry with the butter, then roll up each one, starting with the longest side, and twist into a crescent shape.
3. Put the apricot jam in a mug and warm through for 20 seconds.
4. One at a time, put the croissants in a large mug and microwave for 1 minute until puffed up. Remove from the microwave and brush with the warm jam to glaze.
5. To make the marmalade sauce, put the orange juice, sugar and cloves in a separate large mug and microwave for $1^{1}/2$ minutes, stirring until the sugar has dissolved.

6. Stir well, then microwave for a further minute, watching carefully and pausing if the sauce looks like it is bubbling over.
7. Blend the cornflour to a paste with the butter. Stir it into the sauce and microwave for a further 30 seconds. The sauce is much runnier than a marmalade. Serve with the croissants.

FRENCH TOAST

You need to let the egg and milk soak into the bread for the best results. If you like, assemble it the night before and keep in the fridge to cook in the morning. Those who prefer a savoury option might enjoy it with a dollop of tomato ketchup instead of redcurrant jelly.

---

1 tbsp butter
1 egg
3 tbsp milk
2 slices of bread, cut into cubes
1 tsp redcurrant jelly (optional), to serve

---

1. Put the butter in a mug and microwave for 20 seconds until melted, then swirl it round the inside of the mug.
2. Whisk together the egg and milk in a separate bowl.
3. Gradually layer the bread into the mug, pouring a little of the egg mixture over each piece as you do so. Leave to stand for at least 10 minutes, tipping the mug occasionally so the egg soaks into the bread.
4. Microwave for $1^1/2$ minutes until just firm.
5. Serve with a spoonful of redcurrant jelly, if you like.

PANCAKES AND MAPLE SYRUP

*This is a bit of a cheat, of course, because you can't really make a
pancake in a mug, but it works well and fits in with the spirit of the
book, I think. Try different variations, filling your pancakes with fruit
purée, grated or cream cheese and herbs, or simply lemon and sugar.*

---

2 tsp butter
1 egg
$^1/_2$ cup milk
4 tbsp plain flour
a tiny pinch of salt
2 tsp maple syrup
a squeeze of lemon juice
1 tsp icing sugar, sifted

---

1 Put $^1/_2$ teaspoon of butter on a small microwave plate or the lid of
   a Pyrex dish and microwave for 20 seconds until melted.
2. Whisk together the egg, milk, flour and salt until smooth.
3. Brush the butter over the plate, then pour in about 4 tablespoons
   of the batter so that it covers the plate. Microwave for $1^1/_2$ minutes
   until firm on the top.
4. Flip the pancake over and microwave on the other side for about
   1 minute until firm with bubbles around the edges. Remove from
   the plate and cook 3 more pancakes in the same way.
5. Drizzle the pancakes with maple syrup, roll up, then squeeze a
   little lemon juice over the top and dust with icing sugar.

Herby scrambled eggs with a soda bread roll

Make sure the eggs are still moist when you take them out of the microwave as they will continue to cook for a minute or so after you remove them.

---

5 tbsp plain flour
1 tsp baking powder
a pinch of sugar
1 tbsp natural yogurt
4 tbsp milk or water
1 tsp butter
2 eggs, beaten
salt and freshly ground black pepper
a pinch of chopped fresh parsley

---

1. Put the flour, baking powder, salt and sugar in a large mug. Stir in the yogurt, then gradually add the milk or water to make a soft batter. Microwave for 2–3 minutes until springy to the touch. You'll have a neat little cupcake-size roll.
2. Turn it out of the mug and leave to stand while you make the egg.
3. Put the butter in a clean large mug and microwave for about 20–30 seconds until melted, then swirl it round the inside of the mug.
4. Break the eggs into the mug, whisk lightly and season with salt and pepper. Microwave for 30 seconds.
5. Whisk in the parsley, then microwave for a further 20 seconds.
6. Stir the egg again and microwave for a further 20 seconds until the egg is only just set. Serve with the bread.

HERB OMELETTE STACK

I wasn't going to admit defeat with this one – an omelette in a mug? Why, yes indeed!

---

1 tbsp butter
2 eggs
1 tsp milk
1 tsp chopped fresh parsley, plus extra to garnish
salt and freshly ground black pepper
1 tomato, sliced
tomato ketchup

---

1. Put $^1/_2$ teaspoon of the butter in a mug and microwave for 10 seconds until melted.
2. Whisk together the eggs and milk in a jug. Add the parsley and season with salt and pepper. Pour enough of the mixture to cover the base of the mug and microwave for about 30 seconds until you have an almost-firm mini omelette.
3. Tip the mini omelette onto a plate and keep it warm while you continue to make more omelettes The mixture should make about 6 omelettes.
4. Stack the mini omelettes in a mug, alternating with tomato slices and ketchup, or any other sauces or ingredients of your choice. Garnish with a sprinkling of parsley.

A MUGFUL OF ENGLISH BREAKFAST

Go for broke with this transport-café breakfast.

---

3 tbsp baked beans
1 slice of bread
1 tomato, sliced
1 rasher of bacon, cut into strips
1 chipolata sausage, cut into small chunks
1 egg
tomato ketchup, to serve

---

1. Put the beans in a large mug. Cut the bread to fit the mug and sit it on top, then arrange the tomato slices on top followed by the bacon and sausage chunks. Microwave for 1 minute.
2. Check that the sausages and bacon have not stuck together, then microwave for a further $1^{1}/2$–2 minutes until cooked.
3. Leave to stand while you cook the egg.
4. Line a second mug with clingfilm, leaving the edges hanging over. Break the egg into the mug and pierce the yolk with a cocktail stick. Microwave for 2 minutes until just cooked.
5. Use the clingfilm to help you lift out the egg and put it on top of the sausage. Squeeze a dollop of ketchup on top and dig in.

EGG AND SMOKED BACON BREAKFAST

You can add all kinds of things to this breakfast dish, such as a few peas or some chopped mushrooms.

---

2 rashers of smoked bacon, chopped
1 slice of bread, cut into 2 cm ($^3/_4$ in) squares
1 egg, beaten
tomato ketchup or brown sauce, to serve

---

1. Put the bacon in a large mug and microwave for 45 seconds.
2. Add the bread squares and toss in the bacon fat so the fat soaks into the bread.
3. Break the egg into the mug, whisk lightly, then microwave for 2 minutes until the egg is almost set, whisking occasionally.
4. Leave to stand for 30 seconds, then serve with tomato ketchup or brown sauce.

Soups

This is often the first type of food you think about when quick microwave cooking is mentioned and there are certainly plenty of options. So don't confine yourself to just heating up canned soups. You can use fresh ingredients and make some delicious soups quickly and easily. Since there isn't much space in a mug for the ingredients, it is best to grate vegetables or chop them finely so they cook more quickly and evenly. It is useful to have a hand-held stick blender for some of the soups as it is so easy to simply pop it in the mug and pulse gently until the soup is as smooth as you like. Make sure that you keep the blades of the blender beneath the surface of the liquid so that you don't spray it round the kitchen.

TOMATO AND BASIL SOUP

*If you can keep a pot or two of herbs on your windowsill, you'll have
a ready supply at a fraction of the cost of buying packets of fresh herbs.
If you don't have any fresh basil, just leave it out.*

---

1 tsp olive oil
1 small carrot, finely chopped
$^1/_2$ stick celery, finely chopped
$^1/_4$ tsp finely chopped garlic
1 small can (about 1 cup) chopped tomatoes
$^1/_4$ cup chicken stock
$^1/_4$ tsp dried basil
salt and freshly ground black pepper
a few fresh basil leaves, finely chopped

---

1. Put the oil, carrot, celery and garlic in a large mug and toss to coat
   the vegetables in the oil. Microwave for 1 minute.
2. Add the tomatoes, stock and dried basil and season with salt and
   pepper. Microwave for 1 minute, stir well, then microwave for a
   further 2 minutes in 30-second bursts, stirring between each one,
   until the soup is thick and hot.
3. Blend the soup with a hand-held blender, then top up with boiling
   water if it is too thick. Stir in the fresh basil and season with salt
   and pepper to taste.

Beetroot soup

This makes a coarse-textured soup with a lovely colour. Make sure you buy the cooked beetroot simply vacuum-packed, not stored in vinegar.

---

1 cooked beetroot, chopped
1 tbsp finely chopped onion
$1/4$ tsp finely chopped garlic
$1/2$ cup vegetable stock
freshly ground black pepper
1 tsp soured cream or yogurt

---

1. Put all the ingredients except the cream or yogurt in a large mug and mix together well. Microwave for $1^{1}/2$ minutes until heated through and softened.
2. Purée with a hand-held blender, then check and season with a little more black pepper to taste. Top up with boiling water if necessary.
3. Swirl in the soured cream to serve.

CARROT AND ORANGE SOUP

This quick and easy recipe is super-simple to make, but it still results in a very tasty soup. Serve with crusty bread.

---

1 small can (about 1 cup) carrots, drained and chopped
1/2 cup chicken stock
1 tbsp orange juice
grated zest of 1/2 small orange
a pinch of freshly grated nutmeg
freshly ground black pepper

---

1. Put all the ingredients in a large mug and stir well. Microwave for 1 1/2 minutes.
2. Stir well, then blend to a purée using a hand-held blender.
3. Microwave for a further 1 minute until heated through, making sure the soup does not boil over the top. Top up with boiling water if necessary and stir.

FRENCH ONION SOUP

Although Stilton is far from French, it makes a tasty topping if crumbled over the bread instead of the Brie in this recipe. Banana shallots are larger and a more elongated shape than ordinary shallots but if you can't get them just use two shallots instead.

---

1 banana shallot, thinly sliced into rings
1 tbsp olive oil
$1/4$ tsp finely chopped garlic
$1/2$ tsp dark soft brown sugar
1 tbsp red wine
$1/2$ jellied chicken stock pot
1 slice of bread
3 tbsp chopped Brie or grated Cheddar cheese
salt and freshly ground black pepper
1 tsp chopped fresh parsley

---

1. Put the shallot, oil and garlic in a large mug and microwave for 2 minutes until soft.
2. Stir in the sugar until dissolved, then stir in the wine and jellied stock. Top up to three-quarters full with boiling water, making sure the stock has dissolved. Microwave for 1 minute.
3. Cut a circle of bread the size of the top of the mug and cover it with the cheese.
4. Season the soup with salt and pepper to taste, float the bread on top and sprinkle with the parsley. Leave to stand for 1 minute, then microwave for 1 minute until the cheese has melted and the soup is piping hot. Top up with a little boiling water if necessary.

CHICKPEA SOUP

*Ready-made stock or jellied stock 'cubes' are ideal for this recipe,
although if you have your own stock, that's better still.*

1/2 small can (about 3/4 cup) chickpeas, drained
1/2 cup vegetable stock
a pinch of smoked paprika
freshly ground black pepper

---

1. Put all the ingredients in a large mug and stir well. Microwave for 1 1/2 minutes.
2. Stir well, then blend to a purée using a hand-held blender.
3. Microwave for a further 1 minute until heated through, making sure the liquid does not boil over the top. Top up with boiling water if necessary.

LEEK AND POTATO SOUP

*If you pulse your hand-held blender gently, you'll have no problem using it
straight in the mug and it works surprisingly well to make a thick soup.*

---

1 baby leek, finely chopped
1 rasher of bacon, chopped
1 small potato, peeled and finely chopped
1/2 tsp jellied vegetable stock pot
salt and freshly ground black pepper

---

1. Put the leek, bacon and potato in a large mug and microwave for 1 minute.
2. Stir well, then half-fill the mug with boiling water and stir in the stock. Microwave for 1 minute.
3. Leave to stand for 2–3 minutes until the potato and leeks are soft.
4. Purée using a hand-held blender, then top up with boiling water and season with salt and pepper to taste.

CHICKEN NOODLE SOUP

An all-time favourite, the feel-good factor of this soup depends on the quality of the stock, so use the best that is available.

---

1 cup good-quality chicken stock
$1/2$ nest egg noodles
2 chicken goujons, cut into thin strips
2 tsp sunflower oil
1 spring onion, thinly sliced on the diagonal
$1/4$ tsp finely chopped garlic
a dash of soy sauce
salt and freshly ground black pepper
1 tsp chopped fresh coriander

---

1. Put the stock in a bowl, add the noodles and microwave for 5 minutes until the noodles are tender, stirring twice and ensuring the liquid does not boil over. Drain, reserving the stock.
2. Toss the chicken and oil together in a mug, then microwave for 1 minute. Add the spring onion and garlic and microwave for a further 30 seconds until the chicken is cooked through.
3. Add the noodles and a dash of soy sauce and season with salt and pepper. Fill the mug with the hot stock and sprinkle with coriander.

CHICKEN AND SWEETCORN SOUP

*You'll get the best flavour if you use a good-quality stock. If you don't
make your own, buy some ready-made from the chiller cabinet and
freeze it in ice-cube trays so you can take out just the quantity you need.*

---

1 tsp sunflower oil
2 chicken goujons, chopped
1 tbsp finely chopped onion
$1/4$ tsp finely chopped garlic
$1/4$ cup drained canned or defrosted frozen sweetcorn kernels
$3/4$ cup chicken stock
a pinch of five-spice powder
1 tsp cornflour
$1/2$ egg white, lightly beaten

---

1. Put the oil, chicken, onions and garlic in a large mug and toss to
   coat the ingredients in the oil. Microwave for $1^1/2$ minutes until
   cooked through.
2. Add the sweetcorn, stock and five-spice powder and mix well.
   Microwave for 2 minutes, being careful not to let the soup boil over.
3. Blend the cornflour to a paste with a little cold water and stir it into
   the soup. Microwave for 30 seconds.
4. Stir the soup briskly with a fork as you pour in the egg, so it cooks
   into ribbons that run through the soup.

PEA AND HAM SOUP

This makes a lovely thick and warming soup for winter days.

---

1 tsp sunflower oil
1 shallot, finely chopped, or 2 tbsp finely chopped onion
$1/8$ tsp easy garlic
1 cup frozen peas
1 tbsp chicken or ham bouillon
2 slices cooked ham, chopped
a pinch of sugar
salt and freshly ground black pepper
1 tsp single or double cream

---

1. Put the oil, shallot and chopped garlic in a large mug and microwave for 1 minute.
2. Add the peas and bouillon and half the ham, then top up with boiling water to just cover the peas. Microwave for 2 minutes.
3. Purée the soup using a hand-held blender. If you want a very smooth purée, tip the soup into a fine sieve and rub through into a clean mug.
4. Add the remaining ham and top up with boiling water. Season with a pinch of sugar and salt and pepper to taste.
5. Heat carefully for 30 seconds then stir in the cream and serve.

Eggs and cheese

Eggs are great for quick meals but you do need to be careful not to overcook them otherwise they will go rubbery. Use a variety of different cheeses in your cooking to vary the recipes. You can always personalise recipes depending on what you like and the items you have in the cupboard or the fridge. There are also some egg dishes in the breakfast chapter.

EGGS FLORENTINE

Spinach is frozen in handy blocks that you can use straight from the freezer. You could use steamed fresh spinach, if you prefer, but you'd need to cook it first to reduce it as it's far too bulky for a mug.

---

4 pieces of frozen spinach
$1/4$ tsp finely chopped garlic
salt and freshly ground black pepper
2 tsp double cream
1 slice of bread
1 egg
snipped fresh chives

---

1. Put the spinach and garlic in a large mug and microwave for 1 minute until soft.
2. Stir well and season with salt and pepper. Microwave for a further 2 minutes until the spinach has dried out a little.
3. Stir in the cream and microwave in 30-second bursts for a further $1^1/2$ minutes, stirring between each burst, until the spinach is bubbling hot.
4. Meanwhile, cut a circle of bread just smaller than the diameter of the mug.
5. Put the bread on top of the spinach and press down lightly so the spinach rises up the sides. Break the egg on top and pierce the yolk with a cocktail stick to prevent it exploding. Microwave for 1 minute until almost cooked.
6. Leave to stand for 30 seconds, then sprinkle with chives to serve.

BACON AND EGG QUICHE

Filo pastry will keep for quite a long time in the fridge, or you can freeze it for about 3 months. Do keep it well sealed as otherwise it dries out very quickly and then tends to crumble. This is easiest in a wide mug or cup.

---

1 tbsp butter
1 sheet filo pastry (25 x 45 cm/10 x 18 in), cut into strips
2 rashers of bacon, chopped
2 eggs
2 tbsp milk
salt and freshly ground black pepper
$1/2$ cup grated cheese

---

1. Put the butter in a large, wide mug and microwave for 20 seconds until melted.
2. Lay the pastry on the work surface and brush with the butter. Use the pastry to line the mug, feeding each strip down one side of the mug, then up the other side and overlapping them slightly. Leave the ends overhanging. Microwave for 30 seconds.
3. Put the bacon on a double sheet of kitchen paper and microwave for 2 minutes until just cooked.
4. Whisk together the eggs and milk and season with salt and pepper. Stir in the bacon and cheese, then pour into the cup. Microwave for 5 minutes until just set. Leave to stand for 2 minutes, then serve hot or leave to cool and then chill in the fridge.

Piperade

This is a simple version of the colourful Basque dish of onions, peppers and tomatoes often served, as here, with scrambled egg.

---

1 tsp butter
1 shallot, finely chopped, or 2 tbsp finely chopped onion
1/4 red pepper, deseeded and finely chopped
1/4 green pepper, deseeded and finely chopped
1/4 tsp finely chopped garlic
a dash of Tabasco sauce
salt and freshly ground black pepper
2 eggs, beaten
a little chopped fresh parsley

---

1. Put the butter, shallot, peppers and garlic in a large mug and microwave for 1 minute until softened.
2. Add the Tabasco, salt and pepper to the eggs, then add to the mug and mix well. Microwave for 1 minute.
3. Stir well, then microwave in 30-second bursts, stirring between each burst, for a further 2 minutes until the egg is cooked but still moist.
4. Sprinkle with parsley to serve.

CROQUE MONSIEUR

A croque monsieur is really just a posh name for a cheese and ham toastie! If you like to top it with a poached or fried egg, it becomes a croque madame. If you prefer, you can toast the bread and use squares of toast.

1 slice of bread
2 tsp butter
2 slices of ham, quartered
2 slices of cheese, quartered
freshly ground black pepper

1. Spread the bread with the butter and microwave for about 40 seconds until hot and the butter has melted.
2. Cut the bread into squares or circles to fit the mug. Starting with a piece of bread, layer the ingredients in the mug: bread, ham, cheese, seasoning with a little pepper as you go.
3. Microwave for 1 minute until heated through and the cheese has melted.

PLOUGHMAN'S LAYER

This is a traditional pairing of cheese and pickle but you could also try Brie and caramelised onion, or goats' cheese with a sweet fruit chutney.

2 small slices of bread
2 tsp butter
4 slices strong Cheddar cheese
4 tsp sweet pickle

1. Spread the bread with the butter and cut each piece into quarters.
2. Put 2 pieces of bread in a mug, cover them with a slice of cheese and a spoonful of pickle, then keep layering bread, cheese and pickle until all the ingredients are used.
3. Microwave for $1^1/2$ minutes until bubbling hot.

BEETROOT AND GOATS' CHEESE

Try this tasty combination when you want a light bite at lunchtime – the soft, melted cheese beautifully complements the juicy beetroot. Do remember to buy vacuum-packed cooked fresh beetroot, not the pickled kind.

---

1 small cooked beetroot, sliced
4–6 slices of goats' cheese
freshly ground black pepper
1 tbsp mayonnaise
1 crusty roll, to serve

---

1. Layer the beetroot and cheese slices in a mug and season with black pepper.
2. Microwave for 1–2 minutes until the beetroot is hot and the cheese has melted.
3. Top with a dollop of mayonnaise and serve with a crusty roll.

CAULIFLOWER CHEESE

If you don't like blue cheese, you can use something else, but choose a
strongly flavoured cheese for the best results.

---

1 shallot, finely chopped, or 2 tbsp finely chopped onion
$^1/_2$ rasher of bacon, chopped
1 cup small cauliflower florets
$^1/_2$ cup milk
$^1/_2$ tsp cornflour
$^1/_2$ tsp butter, softened
2 tbsp crumbled Stilton
freshly ground black pepper

---

1. Put the onion and bacon in a mug and microwave for 20 seconds until the onion has softened.
2. Add the cauliflower and milk and microwave for $1^1/_2$ minutes.
3. Turn the cauliflower in the hot milk, then microwave for a further 2 minutes until the cauliflower is just soft.
4. Blend the cornflour and butter together to form a paste, then carefully stir into the milk until thickened. Stir in the cheese and season with pepper. Microwave for 1 minute.
5. Stir well, then microwave for a further 30 seconds until the sauce is thick and coating the cauliflower.

CHEESE FONDUE

A fondue is great fun and with my mug version, you can each have your own. Just leave out the wine, or substitute apple juice, and the kids will love it too.

---

1 tbsp dry white wine
4 tbsp cream or milk
6 tbsp grated Cheddar cheese
$1/2$ tsp cornflour
salt and freshly ground black pepper
chunks of fresh bread and vegetables, for dipping

---

1. Put the wine, 3 tablespoons of the milk and 4 tablespoons of the cheese in a large mug and microwave for 1 minute.
2. Stir well, then microwave for a further 30 seconds until hot and well blended.
3. Mix the cornflour to a paste with the remaining milk, then stir it into the sauce. Microwave for 1 minute until heated through and thickened, watching to make sure it does not boil over.
4. Stir in the remaining cheese and season with salt and pepper to taste. Serve with chunks of fresh bread and vegetables.

Noodles and pasta

As I mentioned at the outset, things like noodles and pasta need to boil vigorously, which is not possible in a mug as there is not enough space to allow the water to bubble up. It is much easier to use a microwave-safe bowl to cook the pasta or noodles and then complete the meal in a mug. However, for those who only have a mug, I have given a mug-method, too. Cooking times will vary, so you may find you'll need to cook for a little longer at step 1.

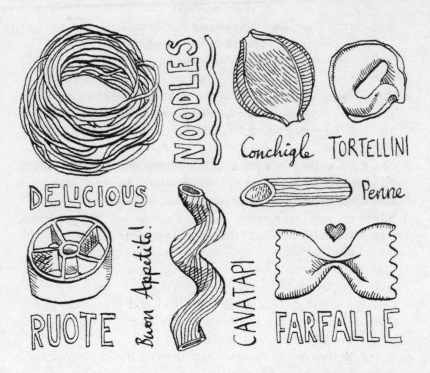

TUNA NOODLES

Cellophane noodles are also known as glass or bean thread noodles because they are almost transparent. You can buy them in any major supermarket.

---

1 nest of cellophane noodles
2 tsp groundnut oil
$^1/_4$ tsp finely chopped garlic
$^1/_4$ tsp chopped ginger root
1 spring onion, chopped
2 baby sweetcorn, cut into chunks
1 tsp soy sauce
1 tsp clear honey
1 small can (about $^1/_2$ cup) tuna, drained and flaked
salt and freshly ground black pepper

---

1. Cut off about 1 tablespoon of the noodles. Soak the remaining noodles in boiling water for 15 minutes, then drain well.
2. Put 1 teaspoon of oil in a large mug and microwave for 20 seconds.
3. Add the dry noodles, stir, then microwave for 10 seconds until puffed up. Stir well, then tip out on to kitchen paper to drain.
4. Add the remaining oil to the mug with the garlic, ginger and onion and microwave for 30 seconds until softened.
5. Add the sweetcorn, soy sauce and honey and stir well. Add the soaked noodles, then stir in about $^1/_4$ cup of boiling water. Microwave for 1 minute to heat through.
6. Stir in the tuna and microwave for a further 1 minute, then season with salt and pepper and serve.

40

BUTTERY EGG NOODLES

If you do something simple but do it really well – it tastes great.
Add some peas, chopped ham or bacon, a litle garlic or chopped peppers
to ring the changes.

---

1 block of egg noodles
1/4 tsp chicken or vegetable jellied stock pot
3 tbsp butter
salt and freshly ground black pepper

---

1. Put the noodles in a large bowl and pour over enough boiling water to cover generously. Stir well, then microwave for 5 minutes until soft, stirring once or twice. Alternatively, put the noodles in a large mug and pour over enough boiling water to cover. Stir well, then microwave for 1 1/2 minutes. Continue to microwave in 30-second bursts for 4 minutes, stirring and topping up with boiling water, as necessary, and being careful not to allow the liquid to boil over. Drain well.
2. Put the drained noodles, stock and butter in a large mug and stir together well. Microwave for 2 minutes until hot.
3. Stir again, season with salt and pepper and leave to stand for 1 minute.

PRAWN POT NOODLES

Play around with the ingredients to suit. This version has a gentle spicy Thai flavour.

---

1 block of egg noodles
a dash of sunflower oil
$1/4$ tsp chopped ginger root
$1/4$ tsp chopped chilli
$1/4$ tsp finely chopped garlic
$1/4$ tsp chopped lemongrass
6 raw peeled prawns
1 tbsp sweetcorn kernels drained from a can or defrosted
$1/2$ cup chicken stock
a dash of fish sauce
a dash of lime juice
1 tsp cornflour
1 tsp chopped fresh coriander

---

1. Put the noodles in a large bowl and pour over enough boiling water to cover generously. Stir well, then microwave for 5 minutes until soft, stirring once or twice. Alternatively, put the noodles in a large mug and pour over enough boiling water to cover. Stir well, then microwave for $1^1/2$ minutes. Continue to microwave in 30-second bursts for 4 minutes, stirring and topping up with boiling water, as necessary, and being careful not to allow the liquid to boil over. Drain well.
2. Put the drained noodles and all the remaining ingredients except the cornflour and coriander in a large mug and stir together well. Microwave for 2 minutes until the prawns turn pink.
3. Mix the cornflour to a paste with a little water, then stir it into the mug and microwave for 1 minute until the sauce thickens.
4. Stir in the coriander and leave to stand for a minute before serving.

SWEET AND SOUR PRAWN NOODLES

Such a popular flavour, this makes a great snack at any time of day.

---

1 block of egg noodles
6–10 raw peeled prawns
2 spring onions, chopped
1 tbsp soy sauce
1 tbsp light soft brown sugar
1 tsp white wine vinegar
2 tsp tomato purée
2 tbsp chicken or vegetable stock
$1/4$ tsp finely chopped garlic

---

1. Put the noodles in a large bowl and pour over enough boiling water to cover generously. Stir well, then microwave for 5 minutes until soft, stirring once or twice. Alternatively, put the noodles in a large mug and pour over enough boiling water to cover. Stir well, then microwave for $1^{1}/2$ minutes. Continue to microwave in 30-second bursts for 4 minutes, stirring and topping up with boiling water, as necessary, and being careful not to allow the liquid to boil over. Drain well and set aside.
2. Put all the remaining ingredients in a large mug and mix together well. Microwave for 2 minutes until hot and the prawns are pink.
3. Stir well, then add the drained noodles and mix together well. Stir in 1–2 tablespoons of boiling water if necessary to make the dish saucier and microwave for 30 seconds.

PASTA IN A CREAMY HERB SAUCE

Soup pasta is available in lots of different shapes – I just happened to have stars in the cupboard.

---

2 tbsp star soup pasta
4 tbsp grated Cheddar cheese
2 tbsp single cream
salt and freshly ground black pepper
2–4 tbsp milk
1 tsp chopped flat parsley

---

1. Put the pasta in a large bowl and pour over enough boiling water to cover generously. Stir well, then microwave for 4 minutes until soft, stirring once or twice. Alternatively, put the pasta in a large mug and pour over enough boiling water to cover. Stir well, then microwave for 1^1/$_2$ minutes. Continue to microwave in 30-second bursts for 3 minutes, stirring and topping up with boiling water, as necessary, and being careful not to allow the liquid to boil over. Drain well.
2. Put the drained pasta in a large mug, add the cheese and cream and stir until well blended. Microwave for 2 minutes until hot.
3. Stir well, season with salt and pepper and add just enough of the milk to get the sauce to the consistency you prefer. Stir in the parsley. Microwave for 1 minute to heat through, if necessary.

SPAGHETTI CARBONARA

I find this easier to eat if the spaghetti is broken into smaller pieces but you can leave it long if you prefer.

---

a handful of spaghetti, broken into pieces
2 slices of pancetta, chopped
$^1/_4$ tsp finely chopped garlic
$^1/_2$ cup single cream
1 egg
2 tbsp grated Parmesan cheese
freshly ground black pepper

---

1. Put the spaghetti in a large bowl and pour over enough boiling water to cover generously. Stir well, then microwave for 5 minutes until soft, stirring once or twice. Alternatively, put the spaghetti in a large mug and pour over enough boiling water to cover. Stir well, then microwave for $1^1/_2$ minutes. Continue to microwave in 30-second bursts for 4 minutes, stirring and topping up with boiling water, as necessary, and being careful not to allow the liquid to boil over. Drain well and set aside.
2. Put the pancetta and garlic in a large mug and microwave for 30 seconds.
3. Stir well, then whisk in the cream, the egg and half the Parmesan. Add the drained spaghetti and stir together well.
4. Microwave for 1 minute until heated through.
5. Sprinkle with the remaining cheese and season to taste with pepper to serve.

PASTA AND PESTO

You can't go wrong with a jar of pesto in the fridge. Stir it into pasta or rice for an almost-instant meal.

---

^{1}/$_2$ cup small macaroni or similar pasta
1–2 tbsp pesto sauce
2 tbsp grated Parmesan cheese
salt and freshly ground black pepper

---

1. Put the pasta in a large bowl and pour over enough boiling water to cover generously. Stir well, then microwave for 5 minutes until soft, stirring once or twice. Alternatively, put the pasta in a large mug and pour over enough boiling water to cover. Stir well, then microwave for 1^1/$_2$ minutes. Continue to microwave in 30-second bursts for 4 minutes, stirring and topping up with boiling water, as necessary, and being careful not to allow the liquid to boil over. Drain well.
2. Put the drained pasta in a large mug, stir in the pesto sauce and half the Parmesan and season with salt and pepper. Microwave for 1 minute until heated through.
3. Sprinkle with the remaining cheese to serve.

MACARONI CHEESE

This classic is comfort in a mug. Try adding some chopped ham or chopped spring onion for extra flavour.

$^1/_2$ cup macaroni
2 tbsp milk or cream
$^3/_4$ cup grated Cheddar cheese
salt and freshly ground black pepper
1 tsp tomato ketchup

---

1. Put the pasta in a large bowl and pour over enough boiling water to cover generously. Stir well, then microwave for 5 minutes until soft, stirring once or twice. Alternatively, put the pasta in a large mug and pour over enough boiling water to cover. Stir well, then microwave for $1^1/_2$ minutes. Continue to microwave in 30-second bursts for 4 minutes, stirring and topping up with boiling water, as necessary, and being careful not to allow the liquid to boil over. Drain well.
2. Put the milk or cream and the cheese in a large mug. Add the drained pasta and season with salt and pepper. Mix together well. Microwave for 2–3 minutes until hot.
3. Top with the tomato ketchup and serve.

Rice and grains

Like pasta, rice needs space to boil, making it tricky to cook in a mug. However, where there's a will, there's a way – so do try these interesting rice dishes. You can stick to the basic 'rules' and use a mug but it's much easier to precook the rice in a bowl before you start. Either way, cook until the rice is just *al dente* – tender to the bite – before moving on. You can also make the recipes with some leftover cooked rice instead, just omitting the first step in each case.

COUS COUS

long grain

Pancetta

BASMATI

KEDGEREE

ARBORIO

PAELLA

Peas

POT PAELLA

Don't worry if you don't have all the ingredients – just use what you have available. If you are using cooked meat, add it at the end and microwave just long enough to heat it through.

$^1/_4$ cup risotto rice
5 cm (2 in) chunk of chicken
1 tbsp finely chopped onion
$^1/_4$ red pepper, deseeded and chopped
$^1/_4$ tsp finely chopped garlic
1 slice pancetta, chopped
1 tsp olive oil
1 chopped mushroom
6 raw peeled prawns
salt and freshly ground black pepper
1 tsp chopped fresh parsley

---

1. Put the rice in a large bowl and pour over enough boiling water to cover generously. Stir well, then microwave for 8 minutes until soft, stirring once or twice. Alternatively, put the rice in a large mug and pour over enough boiling water to cover. Stir well, then microwave for $1^1/_2$ minutes. Continue to microwave in 30-second bursts for 7 minutes, stirring and topping up with boiling water, as necessary, and being careful not to allow the liquid to boil over. Drain well and set aside.
2. Put the chicken, onion, pepper, garlic, pancetta and oil in a mug and mix together well. Microwave for 2 minutes.
3. Stir, then add the mushroom and prawns. Microwave for 1 minute.
4. Stir in the drained rice, then season with salt and pepper. Microwave for 1–2 minutes until the prawns are pink and everything is piping hot.
5. Sprinkle with the parsley to serve.

PRAWN PILAU

Replace the prawns with chopped chicken, button mushrooms
or chunks of firm-fleshed fish for variety.

$^1/_4$ cup risotto rice
1 tsp olive oil
1 shallot, finely chopped, or 2 tbsp finely chopped onion
1 slice of bacon, chopped
$^1/_2$ tsp chilli powder
$^1/_4$ tsp finely chopped garlic
$^1/_2$ cup vegetable stock
1 tsp tomato purée
$^1/_2$ cup raw peeled prawns
salt and freshly ground black pepper
1 tsp cream or crème fraîche
1 tsp chopped fresh parsley

---

1. Put the rice in a large bowl and pour over enough boiling water to cover generously. Stir well, then microwave for 8 minutes until soft, stirring once or twice. Alternatively, put the rice in a large mug and pour over enough boiling water to cover. Stir well, then microwave for $1^1/_2$ minutes. Continue to microwave in 30-second bursts for 7 minutes, stirring and topping up with boiling water, as necessary, and being careful not to allow the liquid to boil over. Drain well.
2. Put the oil, shallot, bacon, chilli and garlic in a large mug and microwave for 1 minute until softened.
3. Add the drained rice and stir to coat it in the oil.
4. Mix together the stock and tomato purée, then add it to the mug with the prawns. Microwave for 2 minutes until the prawns turn pink.
5. Season with salt and pepper and stir in the cream, then sprinkle with the parsley to serve.

RUSHED MUSHROOMS AND RICE

This is an easy way to use leftover rice – either plain or flavoured – to make a quick, tasty supper. Just omit step 1.

---

¹/₄ cup risotto rice
¹/₂ tsp sunflower oil
6 button mushrooms, sliced
2 tbsp crème fraîche or cream
salt and freshly ground black pepper
1 tsp chopped fresh parsley

---

1. Put the rice in a large bowl and pour over enough boiling water to cover generously. Stir well, then microwave for 8 minutes until soft, stirring once or twice. Alternatively, put the rice in a large mug and pour over enough boiling water to cover. Stir well, then microwave for 1¹/₂ minutes. Continue to microwave in 30-second bursts for 7 minutes, stirring and topping up with boiling water, as necessary, and being careful not to allow the liquid to boil over. Drain well and set aside.
2. Put the oil and mushrooms in a large mug and microwave for 1 minute until just soft.
3. Add the cooked rice with the crème fraîche or cream and season with salt and pepper. Microwave for 2 minutes until hot.
4. Sprinkle with the parsley to serve.

KEDGEREE

*This may be a traditional breakfast dish, but it makes a tasty lunch.
If you don't have any cream, just add a little milk or butter.*

---

¹/4 cup long-grain rice
1 egg in its shell
2 tbsp butter
¹/4 tsp curry powder (optional)
1 cooked smoked haddock fillet, skinned and flaked
1–2 tbsp cream
freshly ground black pepper

---

1. Put the rice in a large bowl and pour over enough boiling water to cover generously. Stir well, then microwave for 8 minutes until soft, stirring once or twice. Alternatively, put the rice in a large mug and pour over enough boiling water to cover. Stir well, then microwave for 1¹/2 minutes. Continue to microwave in 30-second bursts for 7 minutes, stirring and topping up with boiling water, as necessary, and being careful not to allow the liquid to boil over. Drain well and set aside.
2. Wrap the egg, in its shell, in kitchen foil. Put the egg in a bowl, cover with boiling water, then microwave for 5 minutes. Leave to stand for 2 minutes, then unwrap, peel and slice or chop roughly.
3. Put the drained rice in a large mug and stir in the butter and curry powder, if using. Gently stir in the haddock, cream and egg and season with pepper to taste. Microwave for 1 minute to heat through.

Savoury rice

You can make this with all kinds of vegetables, so see what you have available and adjust the recipe to suit.

1/4 cup long-grain rice
1 rasher of bacon, chopped
1 shallot, finely chopped, or 2 tbsp finely chopped onion
1/2 red pepper, deseeded and chopped
1 tbsp frozen peas
1/2 cup chicken stock
a pinch of smoked paprika
1 tbsp butter
freshly ground black pepper

---

1. Put the rice in a large bowl and pour over enough boiling water to cover generously. Stir well, then microwave for 8 minutes until soft, stirring once or twice. Alternatively, put the rice in a large mug and pour over enough boiling water to cover. Stir well, then microwave for 1 1/2 minutes. Continue to microwave in 30-second bursts for 7 minutes, stirring and topping up with boiling water, as necessary, and being careful not to allow the liquid to boil over. Drain well.
2. Put the bacon, shallot, pepper and peas in a large mug and microwave for 30 seconds until softened.
3. Add the drained rice and stir until coated in the oil, then stir in the stock and paprika. Microwave for 1 1/2 minutes, watching to make sure it doesn't boil over.
4. Stir in the butter and season with pepper to taste. Leave to stand for 1 minute before serving.

COUSCOUS WITH ROASTED PEPPERS

You can use bulghur wheat prepared in the same way for this dish, if you prefer. I like to toast my couscous before I cook it to give it a nuttier flavour (see page 65).

$^1/_2$ cup couscous, toasted
1 tsp vegetable or chicken jellied stock pot
$^1/_2$ red pepper, deseeded and chopped
2 spring onions, sliced
6 slices of courgette, chopped
$^1/_4$ tsp finely chopped garlic
1 tsp olive oil
1 tsp chopped fresh parsley
salt and freshly ground black pepper

---

1. Put the couscous and concentrated stock in a large mug and half fill with boiling water. Stir well to dissolve the stock, then leave to stand for 5 minutes until the stock has been absorbed, stirring occasionally. Drain off any excess liquid.
2. Put the pepper, spring onions, courgette and garlic in a second mug, drizzle over the oil and stir to coat the vegetables. Microwave for 3 minutes until soft.
3. Mix all the ingredients together, adding the parsley and seasoning with salt and pepper to taste.

Meat and poultry

When cooking in a mug, you need to be careful that meat is thoroughly cooked. Use mince or a finely chopped meat, choosing good-quality cuts that are suitable for quick cooking. If you leave the meat to stand before serving, it will continue to cook, so keep this in mind when you are preparing your meal. You'll be surprised how many interesting and tasty meals you can make in a mug!

BOLOGNESE WITH CIABATTA AND OLIVE OIL

Make sure you chop your ingredients finely for the best results.

---

1 shallot, finely chopped, or 2 tbsp finely chopped onion
$1/4$ tsp finely chopped garlic
1 tsp olive oil
$1/4$ red pepper, deseeded and chopped
3–4 golf ball-sized lumps of minced beef
6–8 tbsp canned chopped tomatoes
$1/2$ tsp tomato purée
a pinch of dried oregano
salt and freshly ground black pepper
1 ciabatta roll
a little extra virgin olive oil, for dipping

---

1. Put the onion, garlic, oil and pepper in a large mug and mix together well. Microwave for 1 minute.
2. Add the meat a little at a time, stirring vigorously to mix it with the vegetables and break up the mince. Microwave for 2 minutes until the meat is coloured.
3. Stir well, then add the tomatoes, tomato purée and oregano and season with salt and pepper. Microwave for a further 1 minute until all the ingredients are hot and well mixed.
4. Leave to stand while you warm the ciabatta roll in the microwave for about 30 seconds and pour some extra virgin olive oil into a little bowl for dipping. Serve with the Bolognese.

CHILLI BEEF

Be cautious with your chilli quantities until you get used to how hot you like this dish. You can also make it with lamb, pork or chicken.

---

1 shallot, finely chopped, or 2 tbsp finely chopped onion
$1/4$ tsp finely chopped garlic
1 tsp olive oil
$1/4$ red pepper, deseeded and chopped
$1/4$ tsp chilli powder, or to taste
$1/4$ cup minced or finely diced beef
6–8 tbsp canned chopped tomatoes
$1/2$ tsp tomato purée
2 tbsp canned red kidney beans
salt and freshly ground black pepper
1–2 flour tortillas

---

1. Put the onion, garlic, oil and pepper in a mug and mix together well. Microwave for 1 minute.
2. Add the chilli and then the meat a little at a time, stirring vigorously to mix it with the vegetables and break up the mince. Microwave for 1 minute until the meat is coloured, then stir vigorously again.
3. Add the tomatoes, tomato purée and kidney beans and season with salt and pepper. Microwave for a further 2 minutes until all the ingredients are cooked through and well mixed.
4. Leave to stand while you warm the tortilla for a few seconds in the microwave and serve with the chilli beef. You can dip the tortilla into the mug and scoop out the beef, if you like.

AMERICAN MEAT LOAF

This is a very simple dish but works surprisingly well. You can make it with lamb, pork or chicken instead of beef if you like.

---

2 tbsp milk
2 tbsp tomato purée
1 shallot, finely chopped, or 2 tbsp finely chopped onions
4 tbsp rolled oats
2 tsp liquid bouillon
1 cup minced beef or finely diced meat
1 tsp tomato ketchup, to serve

---

1. Put all the ingredients except the ketchup in a large mug and mix together well, or blend in a food processor.
2. Microwave for 4 minutes or until the meat is cooked and the dish is hot right through.
3. Leave to stand for 2 minutes, then serve with the ketchup.

GOULASH

Try this mug version of the classic Hungarian casserole.

---

1 tsp olive oil
1 rasher of bacon, chopped
1 shallot, finely chopped, or 2 tbsp finely chopped onion
$1/4$ tsp finely chopped garlic
1 small carrot, chopped
5 tbsp minced beef
$1/2$ tsp paprika
$1/4$ cup canned tomatoes
$1/4$ tsp sugar
salt and freshly ground black pepper
1 tsp soured cream or natural yogurt, to serve

---

1. Put the oil, bacon, shallot, garlic and carrot in a large mug and microwave for $1^1/2$ minutes until softened.
2. Add the beef, paprika, tomatoes and sugar, then season with salt and pepper to taste and mix together well. Microwave for about 2 minutes.
3. Stir everything well, then microwave for a further 2 minutes until the meat is tender and cooked through.
4. Leave the goulash to stand for 1 minute, stir again, then top with the soured cream to serve.

SAUSAGE AND MASH

Sausages can easily overcook, so make sure you don't leave the food in the microwave for too long. If you prefer, simply replace the potatoes with some instant mash for this dish.

---

2 chipolata sausages
1 floury potato, such as Maris Piper, peeled and diced
salt and freshly ground black pepper
1 tbsp butter
tomato ketchup or mustard, to serve

---

1. Pierce the skins of the chipolatas once or twice with a fork. Put them in a large, wide mug and microwave for 2 minutes until just cooked; set aside.
2. Put the diced potato in a bowl, just cover with boiling water and season with a tiny pinch of salt. Microwave for about 5 minutes until the potato is just tender.
3. Drain the potatoes and mash with the butter. Season with salt and pepper to taste and spoon into the mug.
4. Cut the chipolatas into chunks and stir into the potato. Spoon some ketchup or mustard on top to serve.

LAMB WITH APRICOTS

To make a more substantial meal, serve this with a jacket potato.

---

1 tsp oil
1 shallot, finely chopped, or 2 tbsp finely chopped onion
$1/4$ tsp finely chopped garlic
$1/2$ cup lean diced lamb
6 dried apricots, chopped
1 tbsp flaked almonds
$1/4$ tsp ground cumin
1 tbsp tomato purée
$3/4$ cup chicken stock
salt and freshly ground black pepper
1 tsp cornflour

---

1. Put the oil, shallot, garlic and lamb in a large mug and mix together well. Microwave for 2 minutes until the meat is coloured.
2. Drain off any excess fat and stir well, then add all the remaining ingredients except the cornflour, seasoning with salt and pepper to taste. Microwave for 2 minutes.
3. Mix the cornflour to a paste with a little water, then stir it into the mug and microwave for 1–2 minutes until the sauce has thickened.
4. Leave to stand for a minute before serving.

QUICK CHICKEN IN WINE SAUCE

A dash of wine gives this dish extra flavour. You can use red or white – whichever you prefer – or it tastes equally good with apple juice.

1 tsp olive oil
1 shallot, finely chopped, or 2 tbsp finely chopped onion
$1/4$ tsp finely chopped garlic
2 mushrooms, chopped
$1/2$ courgette, diced
2 chicken goujons, cut into thin strips
3 tbsp wine
1 tsp tomato purée
1 tsp cornflour
a pinch of freshly chopped parsley
salt and freshly ground black pepper
$1/2$ tsp torn fresh basil leaves

1. Put the oil, shallot and garlic in a large mug and mix together well. Microwave for 20 seconds until hot.
2. Add the mushrooms, courgette and chicken and mix together well. Microwave for 2 minutes until the chicken is cooked through and the juices are no longer pink.
3. In a separate bowl or mug, whisk together the wine, tomato purée and cornflour, stir in the parsley and season with salt and pepper. Add to the other ingredients and stir well, then microwave for 2 minutes until hot and slightly thickened.
4. Sprinkle with the basil to serve.

CHICKEN FAJITAS

A packet of fajita spices will last ages in the cupboard and make this dish interesting and tasty.

---

2 tbsp thinly sliced onion
$1/4$ tsp finely chopped garlic
$1/2$ tsp olive oil
$1/2$ red pepper, deseeded and very thinly sliced
3–4 chicken goujons, cut into shreds
$1/2$ tsp fajita seasoning
2–3 tbsp chicken stock
freshly ground black pepper
1–2 flour tortillas
guacamole (see page 88), tomato salsa and soured cream, to serve

---

1. Put the onion, garlic, oil, red pepper, chicken and fajita seasoning in a large mug and mix together well. Microwave for $1^1/2$ minutes.
2. Stir well, then microwave for a further $1^1/2$ minutes.
3. Stir again, then add 2 tablespoons of the stock, season with pepper and microwave for 1 minute until the chicken is cooked, adding the remaining stock or a little boiling water if the mixture looks too dry.
4. Leave to stand while you warm the tortillas for a few seconds in the microwave, then serve the chicken with the tortillas, guacamole, salsa and soured cream.

CHICKEN AND CHICKPEA CURRY

*This is a simple and fairly mild curry that you can adapt to suit
your own taste. Add some sliced banana for extra interest.*

$^{1}/_{2}$ tsp olive oil
3 chicken goujons, chopped
1 shallot, finely chopped, or 2 tbsp finely chopped onion
$^{1}/_{4}$ tsp finely chopped garlic
$^{1}/_{2}$ tsp curry powder
2–6 tbsp chicken stock
1 tbsp tomato purée
2 tbsp canned, drained chickpeas
2 tsp sultanas
salt and freshly ground black pepper
1 tbsp cream
naan bread, to serve

---

1. Put the oil, chicken, shallot, garlic and curry powder in a large
   mug and mix together well. Microwave for 1 minute until
   softened.
2. Stir in 2 tablespoons of the stock and the tomato purée and
   microwave for a further 1 minute.
3. Stir again, then add the chickpeas and sultanas, season with salt
   and pepper and microwave for 1 minute until the chicken is
   cooked and the ingredients are all heated through, adding a little
   more stock if necessary to maintain the consistency you prefer.
4. Stir in the cream, then leave the curry to stand while you warm the
   naan in the microwave, then serve.

Fish and seafood

The most important thing when cooking seafood in the microwave is to remember that it cooks very quickly, so err on the side of caution in your cooking times. It is better to undercook then return the food to the microwave for another blast, than to spoil a dish by overcooking.

You can use all kinds of fish for your mug meals but firmer-fleshed varieties will hold together best. Be careful, when stirring, that you don't break up the fish too much.

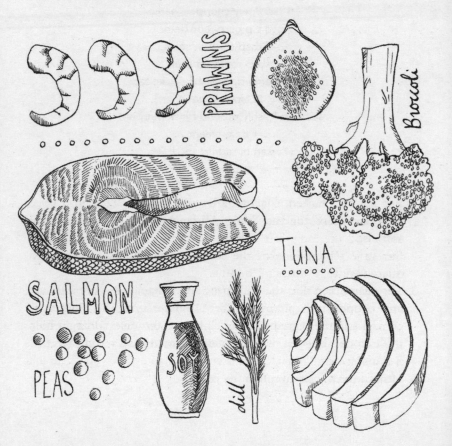

PRAWNS AND COUSCOUS

Toasted couscous has a nuttier flavour, so toast the packet of dry couscous when you buy it, then store it in an airtight jar. To do this, pour the couscous into a dry saucepan over a medium heat and heat for about 5 minutes, stirring and tossing frequently, until the couscous turns a lovely mottled golden brown. Immediately tip it into a bowl and leave to cool. If you just turn off the heat and leave it in the hot saucepan, it's likely to burn.

$^1/_4$ cup couscous, toasted
1 tsp vegetable jellied stock pot
12 raw peeled prawns
1 spring onion, chopped
$^1/_4$ tsp finely chopped garlic
$^1/_4$ red pepper, deseeded and chopped
1 dried fig, chopped
1 tbsp pomegranate molasses or dark soft brown sugar
salt and freshly ground black pepper

---

1. Put the couscous and stock in a mug and pour over boiling water to half fill the mug. Stir well to dissolve the stock, then leave to stand for 5 minutes until the liquid has been absorbed, stirring occasionally.
2. Meanwhile, put the prawns, spring onion, garlic and pepper in a second mug and microwave for 2 minutes. Add the fig and pomegranate molasses, stir well, then microwave for a further 1–2 minutes until the prawns have all turned pink and the pepper is just soft.
3. Mix the prawn mixture into the couscous to serve.

PRAWN RISOTTO

If anyone challenges whether this is actually a risotto, of course they are right – it isn't! But calling the recipes 'risotto-style' or 'almost risotto' would get very boring. In the context of a book about instant meals, I hope I will be forgiven.

---

^{1}/4 cup risotto rice
1 cup vegetable stock
1 tbsp finely chopped onion
1 tsp olive oil
^{1}/4 tsp finely chopped garlic
10 raw peeled prawns
salt and freshly ground black pepper
1 tsp chopped fresh parsley

---

1. Put the rice in a large bowl and pour over enough stock to cover generously. Microwave for 5 minutes until soft, then drain. If you are using a large mug, microwave for 1^1/2 minutes, then continue to microwave in 30-second bursts for 4 minutes, being careful not to allow the liquid to boil over.
2. Put the onion, oil and garlic in a mug and mix together well. Microwave for 1 minute.
3. Stir well, then microwave for a further minute.
4. Stir again, then add the prawns.
5. Drain the rice, then stir it into the mug and season with salt and pepper. Microwave for 1–2 minutes until piping hot and the prawns are pink. Sprinkle with the parsley to serve.

FISH CURRY

Use a good-quality curry powder and choose mild or hot to suit your own taste, or use a curry paste instead.

---

1 tsp sunflower oil
1 shallot, finely chopped, or 2 tbsp finely chopped onion
$1/4$ pepper, deseeded and chopped
$1/2$ tsp finely chopped garlic
2 tbsp frozen peas
$1/8$ tsp curry powder
$1/3$ cup vegetable stock
$1/4$ tsp cornflour
1 small white fish fillet, cut into chunks
3 tbsp yogurt
1 tsp chopped fresh coriander

---

1. Put the oil, shallot, pepper and garlic in a large mug and microwave for 30 seconds until soft.
2. Stir in the peas and curry powder and microwave for 1 minute.
3. Blend together the stock and cornflour, stir into the mug and microwave for 1 minute.
4. Gently stir in the fish, then microwave for 2 minutes until the fish is cooked.
5. Stir in the yogurt and microwave for about 40 seconds to heat through, without allowing it to boil as this will make the sauce split. Sprinkle with the coriander to serve.

SMOKED FISH PIE

Fish pie is among my favourite dishes, so I wanted to include a simplified version in this collection. Use frozen peas instead of the vegetables if you prefer.

⅓ cup milk
1 tsp cornflour
1 tsp tomato purée
3 tbsp butter, softened
2 tbsp chopped frozen mixed vegetables, defrosted
a pinch of mixed herbs
salt and freshly ground black pepper
½–1 smoked fish fillet, such as cobbler, cut into chunks
4 raw peeled prawns
4 tbsp instant mashed potato powder
½ cup boiling water
1 tbsp grated Cheddar cheese
2 tsp crushed cornflakes

---

1. Put the milk, cornflour, tomato purée and half the butter in a large mug and mix together well. Microwave for 1 minute.
2. Add the vegetables and herbs, season with salt and pepper and mix together well. Microwave for 2 minutes.
3. Add the fish and prawns and gently stir into the other ingredients. Microwave for 2 minutes until cooked through.
4. In a separate mug, whisk the mashed potato powder into the boiling water until smooth and thick. Spoon on top of the fish.
5. Mix together the cheese and cornflakes and sprinkle over the top. Microwave for 40 seconds until heated through.

ORIENTAL SALMON

Use a wide cappuccino cup for this simple recipe. It goes well with rice or even instant mashed potato.

---

1 salmon steak
1 tbsp soy sauce
$1/4$ tsp finely chopped garlic
1 spring onion, finely chopped
$1/4$ tsp caster sugar
1 tsp chopped fresh parsley

---

1. Put the salmon in a large, wide mug, cutting it in half or into chunks if necessary. Mix together all the remaining ingredients except the parsley and pour over the salmon. Microwave for about 1 minute.
2. Turn the salmon over and baste with the sauce, then microwave for a further 2 minutes.
3. Turn the fish again and microwave for a further 2 minutes until it is cooked through.
4. Sprinkle with the parsley to serve.

SALMON IN WINE AND DILL

If you use a wide cappuccino cup for this recipe, you can cook the salmon in one piece. Otherwise, cut it into appropriate-sized pieces.

---

1 salmon steak, cut into chunks if necessary
1 tsp butter
freshly ground black pepper
3 tbsp dry white wine
1 tsp chopped fresh dill
1 slice wholemeal bread and butter, to serve

---

1. Put the salmon in a large, wide mug, dot with the butter and season with pepper. Microwave for 2 minutes.
2. Pour over the wine and add the dill. Microwave for about a further 1^1/2 minutes until the salmon is just cooked through.
3. Leave the salmon to stand for 1 minute, then serve with some wholemeal bread

SMOKED HADDOCK WITH RICE AND PEAS

You can rustle up this simple dish when the cupboard is almost bare.

1/4 cup risotto rice
1/4 cup frozen peas
a pinch of cayenne pepper
2 tbsp chicken stock
1 ready-to-eat smoked haddock fillet, skinned and flaked
salt and freshly ground black pepper
1 tsp butter

---

1. Put the rice in a large bowl and pour over enough boiling water to cover generously. Microwave for 8 minutes until soft, then drain. If you are using a large mug, microwave for $1^{1}/2$ minutes, then continue to microwave in 30-second bursts for 7 minutes, being careful not to allow the liquid to boil over.
2. Put the drained rice in a large mug, add the peas, cayenne and stock and microwave for 2 minutes.
3. Stir in the haddock and season with salt and pepper. Microwave for a further 1–2 minutes until heated through, adding a little boiling water if it looks too dry.
4. Stir in the butter before serving.

JACKET POTATO WITH TUNA AND MAYO

You don't need a mug to bake your jacket potato but this is just one of many options to make it more interesting.

---

1 baking potato
1 tbsp butter
1 tbsp mayonnaise
1 tsp tomato ketchup
1 tsp brown sauce
salt and freshly ground black pepper
2 button mushrooms, chopped
1/2 small can (about 3/4 cup) of tuna, drained and flaked
1 tsp snipped fresh chives

---

1. Pierce the potato several times with a fork, then microwave for 6–8 minutes, depending on size, until just soft.
2. Put the butter in a large mug and microwave for 30 seconds until it is just melted.
3. Chop the potato, with its skin, into large bite-sized chunks and put in the mug. Season with salt and pepper, and stir gently to coat the potato in the butter.
4. Meanwhile, mix together the mayonnaise, ketchup and brown sauce and season with salt and pepper. Fold in the mushrooms, then the tuna. Spoon the tuna mayonnaise over the top of the potato and sprinkle with chives to serve.

Vegetables and pulses

Add as much variety as you can by using all kinds of vegetables in your cooking. Locally grown vegetables in season tend to have the best flavour, and for those on a budget, they are great for filling you up as well as being healthy. Have a wander down the vegetable aisle at the supermarket and try out some of the things you may not have even noticed before.

Pick up a few cans of filling, protein-rich pulses, too. Even that old favourite, beans on toast, can be done in a mug – simply cut your toast into chunks and layer it with the beans in a mug before heating them through.

STUFFED MUSHROOM

A single mushroom makes the basis of a very filling little meal. You can also make this with some sage and onion stuffing. I love Stilton but you can use mature Cheddar for a traditional flavour, or a mild Gouda or creamy goats' cheese.

---

1 large mushroom, stalk removed and reserved
3 tbsp vegetable or chicken stock
1 tbsp butter
1 tbsp finely chopped onion
$1/4$ cup breadcrumbs
a generous pinch of chopped sage
salt and freshly ground black pepper
1 tbsp grated Stilton cheese
a few fresh parsley leaves

---

1. Put the mushroom, gill-side up, in a cappuccino cup, spoon over the stock and dot with half the butter. Microwave for 3 minutes until soft. Drain off most of the liquid.
2. Meanwhile, finely chop the mushroom stalk and mix with the onion, breadcrumbs, sage and plenty of salt and pepper.
3. Spoon the stuffing on top of the mushroom, dot with the remaining butter and microwave for $1^1/2$ minutes until the stuffing has softened.
4. Sprinkle with the cheese and microwave for 1 minute until melted. Sprinkle with the parsley to serve.

Honey and mustard mash

Serve this with sausages or grilled meats, or add some chopped cooked ham and top with a fried egg to make a more substantial meal on its own.

---

8 tbsp milk
4 tbsp instant mashed potato powder
2 tsp butter, softened
$1/2$ tsp clear honey
$1/8$ tsp Dijon mustard
salt and freshly ground black pepper

---

1. Put the milk in a large mug and microwave for $1^1/2$ minutes until it is boiling.
2. Whisk in the mashed potato powder, adding boiling water if necessary, until the mixture is smooth.
3. Whisk in the butter until melted, then stir in the honey and mustard and season with salt and pepper to taste.

PEPPER AND CHORIZO POTATOES

If you don't want to watch the potatoes cooking, cook them in a larger bowl for the full 4¹/₂ minutes.

---

1 potato, peeled and diced
¹/₂ cup vegetable stock
6 slices of chorizo sausage, halved
1 tbsp finely chopped onion
¹/₄ tsp finely chopped garlic
freshly ground black pepper
1 tsp chopped fresh parsley

---

1. Put the potato in a large mug and add the stock. Microwave for 2 minutes until hot.
2. Continue to microwave in 20–30-second bursts for a further 2 minutes until the potato is tender, being careful not to allow the water to boil over. Drain well.
3. Put the chorizo, onion and garlic in a second mug and microwave for 1 minute until soft.
4. Stir well, then add to the potato chunks with the parsley and mix together so that the vegetables are coated in the oil from the chorizo. Season with pepper and serve.

SLICED STILTON POTATOES

Use a mandolin, if you have one, to make sure the slices are really thin. For something different, add a chopped slice of cooked ham while you are layering the potatoes.

---

1 tsp olive oil
1 tsp butter
1 potato, peeled and very thinly sliced
1 shallot, finely chopped, or 2 tbsp finely chopped onion
a pinch of dried thyme
salt and freshly ground black pepper
1/4 cup milk
1 tbsp Stilton or other blue cheese, crumbled

---

1. Put the oil and butter in a large mug and microwave for about 20 seconds until melted.
2. Put the potato and shallot in a bowl, pour over the oil and butter mixture, add the thyme and season with salt and pepper to taste. Toss together to mix the ingredients and coat in the fat.
3. Spoon the mixture back into the first mug and pour in the milk. Microwave for 3 minutes, being careful not to allow the milk to boil over. Check that the potatoes are tender; if not, microwave for a further 2 minutes.
4. Sprinkle over the crumbled cheese and microwave for 30 seconds until it has melted.

PEPPERS AND FENNEL WITH ORANGE

Depending on the size of your vegetables and how much room you have in your mug, you may need to use slightly fewer veggies, so don't worry if you don't have all the listed ingredients.

---

2 slices aubergine, diced
1/2 red pepper, deseeded and diced
1/2 yellow pepper, deseeded and diced
1 shallot, finely chopped, or 2 tbsp finely chopped onion
1 small fennel bulb, thinly sliced
1/2 tsp finely chopped garlic
1/2 small courgette, diced
2 tbsp olive oil
1 small can (about 3/4 cup) chopped tomatoes
grated rind and juice of 1/2 small orange
salt and freshly ground black pepper

---

1. Put the vegetables in a large mug, drizzle with the olive oil and toss together well. Microwave for about 3 minutes until soft, stirring occasionally to ensure they cook evenly.
2. Stir in the tomatoes, orange rind and juice, then season with salt and pepper to taste. Microwave for 3 minutes until hot, stirring occasionally.

PARSNIP AND TOMATO SLICES

Parsnips cook quickly when grated, making them ideal for mug meals as you can enjoy that lovely sweet flavour. Make the dish rich and creamy with a drop of any type of cream, or just add a little vegetable stock.

---

1 parsnip, peeled and grated
1 small can (about 1 cup) chopped tomatoes
1 rasher of bacon, chopped (optional)
a pinch of sugar
salt and freshly ground black pepper
3 tbsp cream
2 tbsp grated Cheddar cheese
1 savoury cracker, crushed
1 tbsp butter

---

1. Put one-third of the parsnip in the bottom of a large mug.
2. Mix together the tomatoes and bacon, if using, then season with sugar, salt and pepper. Spoon one-third on top of the parsnips, then spoon in 1 tablespoon of the cream.
3. Repeat the layers twice more.
4. Mix together the cheese and cracker and sprinkle over the top, then dot with butter. Microwave for 5 minutes until cooked through and tender.

JACKET POTATO WITH SPICY BEANS

Canned pulses make a great standby in the cupboard.

---

1 baking potato
$^1/_2$ tsp olive oil
$^1/_2$ red pepper, deseeded and chopped
1 shallot, finely chopped, or 2 tbsp finely chopped onion
1 small can (about 1 cup) refried beans
$^1/_2$ tsp chilli powder
1 tsp tomato purée
salt and freshly ground black pepper
1 tbsp butter

---

1. Pierce the potato several times with a fork, then microwave for 6–8 minutes, depending on size, until just soft.
2. Put the oil, pepper and shallot in a large mug and toss together until well mixed. Microwave for 1 minute until soft.
3. Add the refried beans, chilli and tomato purée, season with salt and pepper to taste and mix together well. Microwave for about 3 minutes until heated through.
4. Put the potato in a wide cup. Cut a cross in the top of the potato, mash in the butter and season with salt and pepper.
5. Spoon the hot beans over the top and serve.

PEASE PUDDING POCKETS

Quick and easy to heat up, this makes a great snack with extra mango chutney. Adjust the quantities to suit your appetite and your taste.

---

1 small can (about 1 cup) pease pudding
$1/2$ tsp curry powder
2 tbsp mango chutney, plus extra to serve
freshly ground black pepper
1 naan bread
2 cherry tomatoes, halved
a few salad leaves

---

1. Put the pease pudding into a large mug and stir to break it up into chunks. Microwave for 2 minutes to warm through.
2. Stir in the curry powder and mango chutney, then microwave for a further 3 minutes until piping hot.
3. Season with pepper to taste.
4. Warm the naan in the microwave for 30 seconds.
5. Tear the naan into strips and use to scoop out the pease pudding and serve with the tomatoes and lettuce and some extra chutney, if you like.

Salads

You can make some delicious and healthy salads just by tossing a few key ingredients into a mug. The key is not to make your salads too complicated, and to prepare your ingredients in quite small chunks so they are easy to mix together and easy to eat. Always remember that any recipe is only a guide – you can always add or subtract ingredients to work with what you have or to make the most of your particular favourite flavour combinations.

LITTLE GEM

avocado

TOMATO

BALSAMIC Vinegar

MINT

COUSCOUS, CORN AND PEPPER SALAD

Couscous gives bulk to a salad and is ideal for lunch-box choices.

1/4 cup couscous, toasted (see page 65)
1 small shallot, finely chopped
1/4 tsp vegetable jellied stock pot
1/4 small red pepper, deseeded and chopped
2.5 cm (1 in) piece of cucumber, chopped
1 tbsp sultanas
1 tbsp sweetcorn kernels
freshly ground black pepper
1 tsp chopped fresh parsley
1 tsp extra virgin olive oil

---

1. Put the couscous and shallots in a large mug, add the stock. Dissolve the stock pot in the boiling water and pour enough over the couscous to cover. Stir well, then leave to stand for 10 minutes until the liquid has been absorbed, stirring occasionally.
2. Stir in the peppers, cucumber, sultanas and sweetcorn. Season with a little pepper and finish with a sprinkling of fresh parsley and a drizzle of oil.

MIXED GREEN SALAD

Although you can buy bags of mixed salad, they tend to be quite expensive and once opened they don't last very long. Try buying smaller quantities of two or three items and combining them in imaginative ways.

1/2 little gem lettuce, torn into shreds
2 cherry tomatoes, halved
2 spring onions, sliced
a few slices of courgette, cucumber, radish or beetroot
2 tbsp olive oil
1 tsp balsamic vinegar
1/4 tsp Dijon mustard
a pinch of sugar
salt and freshly ground black pepper

---

1. Mix together the lettuce, tomatoes, spring onions and other vegetables in a large mug.
2. Whisk together the oil, vinegar and mustard until emulsified, then season with salt and pepper. Drizzle over the salad and toss together to serve.

AVOCADO AND WARM PANCETTA SALAD

Prepare the avocado just before you serve it to prevent it from going brown.

---

1 slice of pancetta, chopped
$1/2$ avocado, peeled, stoned and sliced
a handful of lambs' lettuce leaves
1 tsp pumpkin seeds
a squeeze of lemon juice
freshly ground black pepper
1 tsp olive oil
$1/2$ tsp balsamic vinegar

---

1. Put the pancetta in a large mug and microwave for 1 minute until crisp. Tip out on to a plate.
2 Put the avocado, lettuce and pumpkin seeds in the mug. Squeeze in the lemon juice and season with pepper.
3. Whisk together the oil and vinegar and drizzle over the salad. Top with the pancetta and serve.

ONION, CARROT AND MINT SALAD

Soak the onion in boiling water for 5–10 minutes to soften the flavour, then drain, or you can simply use raw onion if you prefer.

---

1 onion, thinly sliced
1 carrot, grated
2 tbsp chopped fresh mint leaves
1 tbsp olive oil
$3/4$ tsp white wine vinegar
$1/4$ tsp Dijon mustard
a pinch of sugar
sea salt and freshly ground black pepper

---

1. Put the onion (softened in boiling water, see above, if you wish), carrot and mint leaves in a large mug and mix together well.
2. Whisk together the oil, wine vinegar, mustard and sugar until emulsified, then season with salt and pepper to taste.
3. Drizzle the dressing over the salad and toss together well.

CARROT AND BEETROOT SALAD

*For a different texture, replace the raw beetroot with matchstick-sized
pieces of cooked beetroot.*

---

1 large carrot, grated
1 raw beetroot, peeled and grated
1 shallot, very thinly sliced
2 tsp sultanas
1 tbsp olive oil
1 tsp balsamic vinegar
$1/4$ tsp sugar
$1/4$ tsp mustard

---

1. Put the carrot, beetroot and shallot in a large mug and mix
   together well.
2. Add the sultanas and stir again.
3. Whisk together the oil, vinegar, sugar and mustard. Pour over the
   salad and toss together to serve.

GUACAMOLE

You can serve this as a dip with sticks of carrot, celery or pitta bread,
or as an accompaniment to other dishes, such as chicken fajitas.

---

1 avocado
1 tsp lime juice
$^1/_2$ garlic clove, crushed
1 tbsp mayonnaise
salt and freshly ground black pepper
tortilla chips, to serve

---

1 Peel and stone the avocado. Chop the flesh and put it in a large
   mug. Either purée with a hand-held blender or, if you prefer a
   rougher texture, mash with a fork.
2. Stir in the lime juice, garlic and mayonnaise and season with salt
   and pepper.
3. Serve with tortilla chips.

SWEET TOMATO SALAD

This salad is best if you can leave it to stand for a while before serving.

---

2 tomatoes, thinly sliced
1 tbsp caster sugar
freshly ground black pepper
2 tbsp olive oil
1 tsp white wine vinegar

---

1. Layer the tomatoes in a large mug, sprinkling with sugar and a little pepper as you go.
2. Whisk together the oil and white wine vinegar and pour the dressing over the tomatoes.
3. Leave to stand for at least 30 minutes before serving.

Desserts

It's fun to treat yourself to a dessert now and again, or simply to enjoy some fruit or yogurt. This section includes both hot and cold options, all of which can be enjoyed straight from the mug, although the portions are fairly generous so you may want to tip them out of the mug to share. The selection includes some that may surprise you, so you'll have plenty of variety, from a simple crème caramel to an utterly indulgent chocolate pudding.

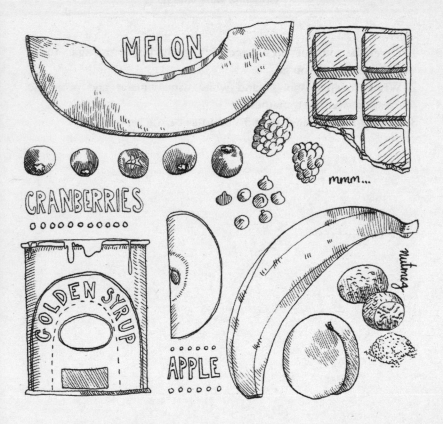

MELON WITH RASPBERRY CREAM DIP

You can make this in minutes with any combination of soft fruits.
It's great for using up the last of a pot of cream – any kind will do.

$^1/_2$ mug raspberries
1 tbsp dry white wine
4 tbsp single cream
a dash of balsamic vinegar
$^1/_4$ melon, cut into chunks

---

1. Put the raspberries, wine and cream into a large mug. Purée with a hand-held blender until smooth.
2. Add the balsamic vinegar and stir through.
3. Serve the raspberry dip with the chunks of melon to dip in.

CRÈME CARAMEL

Allow a little time for your caramel custard to set and you will have a very stylish dessert.

---

2 tbsp water
$2^{1}/_{2}$ tbsp demerara sugar
1 egg
$^{1}/_{3}$ cup milk
1–2 tsp caster sugar

---

1. Put the water and demerara sugar in a large mug and microwave for 2 minutes until it turns to caramel.
2. Whisk the egg with the milk and caster sugar, then strain into the mug, pouring down the side to avoid disturbing the caramel. Microwave for 3 minutes until just set.
3. Leave to stand for about 2 minutes, then chill the dessert thoroughly. When you are ready to eat, turn it out onto a plate and serve.

CRANBERRY COMPOTE

This makes a lovely dessert with a little natural yogurt, or a fabulous breakfast if you spoon it over porridge. Vary the fruits and nuts according to what you have in the cupboard. Allow time for it to cool.

---

2 tbsp dried cranberries
3 stoned prunes, quartered
2 tbsp sultanas or raisins
2 soft dried figs, quartered
6 ready-to-eat dried apricots, halved
$1/4$ tsp grated lemon zest
1 tbsp dark soft brown sugar
2 tbsp boiling water

---

1. Put all the ingredients in a large mug and microwave for 1 minute.
2. Stir well, then microwave for a further 2 minutes until the fruit is soft and coated in a light syrup. Add a little more boiling water if the mixture is too thick.
3. Leave to cool, stirring occasionally, before serving.

APPLE AND BLACKBERRY NUTMEG CRUMBLE

You can use a small cooking apple for this dish but the result will be softer and you may need a little more sugar. Any type of cream, crème fraîche or even yogurt will taste good.

---

1 crisp eating apple, peeled, cored and thinly sliced
2 tbsp blackberries
6 tbsp rolled oats
2 tbsp plain flour
2 tbsp dark soft brown sugar
a pinch of freshly grated nutmeg
1–2 tbsp butter, finely diced
1 tsp cream

---

1. Put the apple slices in a large mug and microwave for 1 minute until beginning to soften.
2. Stir in the blackberries. Mix together the oats, flour, sugar, nutmeg and butter, then sprinkle them over the apple. Microwave for 2 minutes.
3. Leave to cool for 5 minutes then top with a spoonful of cream to serve.

Syrup Pudding with Warm Caramel Sauce

This is the classic steamed syrup pudding – so easy to make in the microwave.

---

2 tbsp golden syrup
4 tbsp butter
4 tbsp light soft brown sugar
1 egg, beaten
4 tbsp plain flour
$1/4$ tsp baking powder

For the sauce
1 tbsp butter
2 tbsp dark soft brown sugar
1 tbsp golden syrup

---

1. Put the syrup in a large mug.
2. Mix together the remaining pudding ingredients in a bowl and then spoon into the mug. Microwave for 2–3 minutes until risen and springy to the touch.
3. Leave to stand while you make the sauce.
4. For the sauce, put the butter, sugar and syrup in a second large mug and microwave for 30 seconds until melted.
5. Stir vigorously until the sauce is smooth and no longer grainy.
6. Pour over the pudding to serve.

STICKY TOFFEE PUDDING

We could hardly produce a book without a version of everyone's favourite!

---

2 soft dried figs, chopped
2 tbsp water
4 tbsp butter, softened
$1/4$ tsp ground cinnamon
4 tbsp dark soft brown sugar
4 tbsp plain flour
$1/4$ tsp baking powder
1 egg
5 cm (2 in) piece of caramel chocolate bar

---

1. Put the figs and water in a large mug and microwave for 1 minute until soft, then squash against the sides of the mug.
2. Add the remaining ingredients except the caramel chocolate bar to the mug and mix to a soft batter. Microwave for 2–3 minutes until risen and springy to the touch. Leave to stand while you make the sauce.
3. Break up the caramel chocolate bar and put it in a second mug and microwave for 30 seconds.
4. Stir well, then microwave for a further 30 seconds.
5. Stir until the chocolate is completely melted and smooth. Pour over the dessert to serve.

CHOCOLATE AND WHITE CHOCOLATE CHIP PUDDING

If you use a large cappuccino cup for this recipe, you'll make a cute individual pudding that you can turn out and enjoy in style – whether you are making just one for yourself or several to share with friends. Use milk or white chocolate chips if you prefer. Allow time for it to cool.

---

2 tbsp plain flour
$1/4$ tsp baking powder
1 tsp cocoa powder
2 tsp dark soft brown sugar
1 tbsp white chocolate chunks
1 tbsp sunflower oil
1 small egg, beaten
1 tbsp crème fraîche, to serve

---

1. Put all the dry ingredients including the chocolate in a large, wide mug or cappuccino cup and stir together well. Add the oil and egg and stir again. Microwave for 2 minutes until risen and springy to the touch.
2. Leave to stand for 1 minute. Serve warm from the cup or turn out on to a plate, topping with crème fraîche.

CRANBERRY AND MAPLE SYRUP BREAD AND BUTTER PUDDING

Use sultanas instead of cranberries and ordinary syrup or sugar in place of maple syrup if you don't have all the ingredients.

---

2 slices bread
2 tbsp butter, softened
1 egg
1/2 cup milk
6 tbsp dried cranberries
1 tbsp maple syrup

---

1. Spread the bread with the butter, then cut each slice into 16 squares.
2. Whisk together the egg and milk in a small bowl.
3. Put a layer of bread in the bottom of a large mug, sprinkle with a few of the cranberries and a little of the maple syrup, then pour over a little of the egg mixture.
4. Continuing layering the ingredients and pouring over the egg until you have used all the ingredients, finishing with a layer of bread and butter.
5. Leave to soak for at least 10 minutes, preferably 30 minutes.
6. Microwave for 4 minutes, then leave the pudding to stand for about 1 minute before eating.

BANOFFEE DESSERT

You can serve this warm or cold, but do be careful when it is first out of the microwave as it will be very hot.

---

1 tbsp butter
2 tbsp dried breadcrumbs
$1/2$ banana, sliced
$1/2$ cup condensed milk
1 tsp demerara sugar

---

1. Put the butter in a mug and microwave for 20 seconds until it is melted.
2. Stir in the breadcrumbs. Place the banana slices on top and pour over the condensed milk. Microwave for 1 minute.
3. Microwave in 15-second bursts for a further 2–3 minutes, watching to make sure the milk does not boil over. It will bubble up and mix the layers together, turning golden brown in the process.
4. Leave to cool for at least 10 minutes. Sprinkle with the sugar and serve warm, or leave to cool and chill before serving.

RICE PUDDING

Rich and creamy and so simple to make, serve this with a drizzle of honey or a dollop of your favourite jam. You can also make a nice pudding with ground rice (see next recipe).

---

2 tbsp pudding rice
1 tbsp caster sugar
1 tbsp butter
$^1/_2$ cup milk, plus extra if necessary
1 tsp clear honey or fruit jam, to serve

---

1. Put the rice in a large bowl and pour over enough boiling water to cover generously. Microwave for 8 minutes until soft, then drain. If you are using a large mug, microwave for $1^1/_2$ minutes, then continue to microwave in 30-second bursts for 7 minutes, being careful not to allow the liquid to boil over.
2. Put the drained rice and all the remaining ingredients except the honey or jam in a large mug and microwave for $1^1/_2$ minutes.
3. Stir well, then leave to stand for 2 minutes.
4. Microwave in 30-second bursts for a further 4 minutes, stirring between each burst.
5. Leave to stand for 2 minutes, then serve with honey or jam.

Semolina or Ground Rice Pudding

To make this more indulgent, try stirring a spoonful of cream into the finished dessert, if you have some.

---

2 tbsp semolina or ground rice
2 tsp sugar
1–1¼ cups milk
a few drops of vanilla extract
1 tsp jam, honey or syrup

---

1. Put the semolina or ground rice, sugar and 1 cup milk in a large mug and mix together until smooth. Microwave for 1½ minutes.
2. Add the vanilla and whisk again, making sure there are no lumps. Microwave for 1 minute.
3. Whisk in most of the remaining milk, then microwave in 20-second bursts for a further 2 minutes, whisking between each burst and making sure the liquid does not boil over the top of the mug.
4. Top up with the remaining milk, if necessary, to achieve a smooth consistency, and whisk until well blended, then finish with a spoonful of jam, honey or syrup.

Cakes and cookies

Many of these cakes also work as puddings, so you can serve them hot as a dessert – perhaps with a little cream – or cold as a cake with a cup of tea.

You may find it preferable to mix with a knife or a fork, rather than a spoon, as it is easier to get into the corners of the mug and make sure you have mixed all the ingredients together. If you use a wide mug or a cappuccino cup, you will find that your cakes cook more evenly. If your mug is too tall, you could find that the bottom of the cake goes rather hard. As with the desserts, you can eat them from the mug or run a knife around the edge of the mug and turn them out on to a plate to serve.

Finally, you may like to try making the world's fastest chocolate cake (well, perhaps not officially but it must be in the running). Mix 5 tablespoons of self-raising flour, 5 tablespoons of chocolate and nut spread, 3 tablespoons of mayonnaise (trust me!) and 1 egg in a mug, then microwave for 3 minutes. And that's it!

STRAWBERRY CHEESECAKE

This makes a lovely cheesecake with a sharp tang of lemon. Allow time for it to cool and chill.

---

3 tbsp cream cheese
1 egg
$^{1}/_{2}$ tsp lemon juice
$^{1}/_{4}$ tsp vanilla extract
2 tbsp caster sugar
a few strawberries, sliced
1 tbsp double or whipping cream, whipped
1 tsp chopped nuts

---

1. Put the cheese, egg, lemon juice, vanilla and caster sugar in a large mug and mix together well. Microwave in 30-second bursts for $1^{1}/_{2}$ minutes, stirring after each burst.
2. Whisk again – the mixture will still be very soft – then cool. Chill in the fridge until ready to serve.
3. Arrange the strawberries on top, spoon over the cream and sprinkle with chopped nuts to finish.

Egg custard

You can leave out the pastry and just make the custard if you prefer.
I found it easier to make this in a cappuccino cup.

---

1 tbsp butter
1/2 sheet filo pastry, cut into strips
2 eggs, beaten
1/2 cup cream
2 tsp cornflour
freshly grated nutmeg

---

1. Put the butter in a large, wide mug or cappuccino cup and microwave for 20–30 seconds until melted.
2. Place the filo pastry strips on a work surface and brush them with the melted butter. Line the mug with the strips, overlapping them slightly and leaving a little overhanging at the top. Microwave for 40 seconds.
3. Beat together the eggs, cream and cornflour until smooth. Pour into the cup and sprinkle with the nutmeg. Microwave for about 3 minutes until just set.
4. Leave to cool, then chill before eating.

Whisky tea bread

A fruity little tea bread, serve this sliced and spread with butter or just on its own.

---

4 tbsp plain flour
1 tbsp sultanas
1 tbsp chopped dates
1 egg
2 tbsp cold tea
1 tsp whisky
1 tsp butter, softened
2 tbsp dark soft brown sugar
1 tbsp clear honey
1/4 tsp baking powder
1/4 tsp mixed spice

---

1. Put all the ingredients into a large mug and stir together well to form a smooth batter. Microwave for 2–3 minutes until risen and springy to the touch.
2. Leave to stand for 1 minute, then turn out of the mug so that it cools more quickly and serve sliced and buttered.

Honey and almond cake

Sweet and simple, this is a lovely, light cake.

---

4 tbsp ground almonds
4 tbsp plain flour
1 egg
2 tbsp butter, softened
$1/2$ tsp baking powder
2 tbsp clear honey, plus 1 tsp for drizzling

---

1. Put all the ingredients except the drizzling honey in a large mug and mix together well. Microwave for 3 minutes.
2. Spoon over the remaining honey and leave it to soak in.

Lemon drizzle cake

I like lemon-flavoured things to really taste of lemon, so you may find you prefer to reduce the quantity of lemon juice and zest in this recipe. It will cool more quickly if you turn it out of the mug.

---

3 tbsp butter, softened
2 tbsp caster sugar
1 egg
4 tbsp plain flour
$1/4$ tsp baking powder
grated zest and juice of $1/2$ lemon
2 tsp icing sugar

---

1. Put all the ingredients except the lemon juice and icing sugar in a large mug and mix together well.
2. Add half the lemon zest and a few drops of lemon juice and mix again. Microwave for 3 minutes until the cake is risen and springy to the touch.
3. Blend together the remaining lemon zest and juice with the icing sugar. Spoon over the cake and leave to cool before serving.

SQUIDGY CHOCOLATE CAKE

Everyone loves a chocolate cake, and this is so easy, quick and delicious, you'll soon be coming back for more.

---

4 tbsp self-raising flour
4 tbsp light soft brown sugar
1 egg
1 tbsp cocoa powder
3 tbsp chocolate and nut spread
1 tbsp milk
1 tbsp sunflower oil

---

1 Put all the ingredients in a large mug and mix together well.
2. Microwave for 2–3 minutes until risen and springy to the touch. The cake should be shiny on the top.
3. Leave to cool before serving.

Coffee cake

*Try this with a little coffee icing, made by beating together
a teaspoon of butter with 2 teaspoons of icing sugar and $1/4$ teaspoon
of instant coffee powder.*

---

3 tbsp butter
3 tbsp dark soft brown sugar
3 tbsp ground almonds
1 tbsp plain flour
$1/2$ tsp baking powder
1 egg, beaten
1 tsp instant coffee powder or crushed granules

---

1. Put the butter in a large mug and melt in the microwave for about 30 seconds.
2. Add all the remaining ingredients and whisk together well. Microwave for 3 minutes until risen and springy to the touch.
3. Leave to cool before serving.

CARROT CAKE WITH CREAM CHEESE ICING

A little bit of icing makes this extra special.

---

3 tbsp butter
3 tbsp plain flour
$1/4$ tsp baking powder
2 tbsp dark soft brown sugar
1 carrot, grated
1 egg, beaten
a pinch of ground cinnamon
1 tbsp cream cheese
4 tbsp icing sugar, sifted

---

1. Put the butter in a mug and microwave for 15 seconds until it is softened, but not melting.
2. Mix in the flour, baking powder, sugar, carrot, egg and cinnamon until smooth. Microwave for 3 minutes until risen and springy to the touch. Leave to cool.
3. Blend together the cream cheese and icing sugar until smooth and spread over the top of the cake.

ALMOND AND MUSCOVADO CAKE

If you use a gluten-free baking powder, this is suitable for those with a gluten intolerance. It will bubble quite high up the mug, so use the largest mug you have and check after 2 minutes to make sure the mixture doesn't bubble over, pausing to let it subside before finishing.

---

4 tbsp butter, softened
4 tbsp ground almonds
$^1/_8$ tsp baking powder
4 tbsp dark muscovado sugar
1 egg
1 tbsp flaked almonds

---

1. Put all the ingredients except the flaked almonds in a very large mug and mix together well. Sprinkle with the flaked almonds. Microwave for 3 minutes until risen and spongy and bubbly on top.
2. Served warm or cold, this is a soft-textured cake that is best eaten with a fork.

FUDGE CHUNK MUGMUFFIN

Stand the mug on a piece of kitchen paper on the microwave turntable. Because the mixture rises up – like the top of a normal muffin – it can spill over slightly if your mug is a different size, so the paper will make any clearing up easier.

---

6 tbsp plain flour
1 tbsp cocoa powder
1/4 tsp baking powder
5 tbsp dark soft brown sugar
1 egg
4 tbsp sunflower oil
2 tbsp fudge chunks
a little cream (optional), to serve

---

1. Put all the ingredients except the fudge and cream in a large mug and mix together well. Stir in the fudge. Microwave for 3 minutes until risen and springy to the touch but still slightly moist.
2. Serve hot with cream, or cold just on its own.

MOCHA CAKE WITH
WARM CHOCOLATE SAUCE

Add a little milk if the mixture seems too stiff. You can leave the cake in
the mug or turn it out – either way, it's delicious.

---

4 tbsp butter, softened
1 egg
4 tbsp plain flour
$1/4$ tsp baking powder
1 tbsp cocoa powder
3 tbsp dark soft brown sugar
$1/2$ tsp coffee powder or crushed granules
1 tsp icing sugar, sifted

For the sauce
1 tbsp butter
2 tbsp dark soft brown sugar
1 tbsp golden syrup
2 squares of dark chocolate

---

1. Put all the cake ingredients except the icing sugar in a large mug and mix together well. Microwave for 3 minutes until risen and springy to the touch.
2. Leave to cool.
3. For the sauce, put the butter, sugar and syrup in a mug and microwave for 30 seconds until melted.
4. Stir vigorously until the sauce is smooth and no longer grainy. Add the chocolate and microwave for 30 seconds until the chocolate is beginning to melt.
5. Stir vigorously until the chocolate has melted completely and blended into the sauce. Pour over the cake to serve.

PEANUT BUTTER AND JELLY CAKE

Peanut butter and jelly is a classic combination in the United States that's becoming more popular around the world. Crunchy or smooth will obviously give you slightly different textures – take your pick.

---

6 tbsp plain flour
1/4 tsp baking powder
3 tbsp sunflower oil
3 tbsp peanut butter
1 egg
2 tbsp caster sugar
2 tbsp redcurrant jelly, plus extra to serve (optional)

---

1. Put all the ingredients into a large mug and mix together well. Microwave for 3 minutes until risen and springy to the touch.
2. Top with a little more redcurrant jelly, if you like.

BANANA LOAF

*You can always make this simple loaf cake to use up the last banana in
the bowl that has just started to go a little soft.*

---

1 tbsp butter, softened, plus extra for spreading
1 banana, mashed
1 egg
4 tbsp strong plain flour
3 tbsp sunflower oil
1/4 tsp baking powder
2 tbsp dark soft brown sugar

---

1. Put all the ingredients in a large mug and mix together well.
   Microwave for 3 minutes until risen and springy to the touch.
2. Leave to stand for 2 minutes, turn out of the mug and serve warm
   or cooled, sliced and buttered.

TEA CAKE BAKE

Try this tea cake turned out of the mug, then sliced and buttered.

$^{1}/_{4}$ – $^{1}/_{2}$ cup milk
$^{2}/_{3}$ cup plain flour
$^{1}/_{2}$ tsp baking powder
$^{1}/_{2}$ tsp mixed spice
2 tbsp caster sugar
1 tsp butter, softened
2–3 tbsp sultanas
1 tsp jelly conserve or apricot jam, sieved

---

1. Put all the ingredients except the jam into a large mug and mix together to a slightly stiff dough. Microwave for $2^{1}/_{2}$ minutes until slightly damp on the top.
2. Brush the top with the jelly or jam and microwave for a further 30 seconds until risen, shiny and springy to the touch.
3. Leave for 1 minute, then turn out, leave to cool completely and serve sliced and buttered.

CHOCOLATE CRUMBLE COOKIE WITH HOT CHOCOLATE

Total indulgence at its best – you'll need to throw away the calorie rule book when you try this experience.

---

1 tbsp butter
1 tbsp demerara sugar
1 tbsp dark soft brown sugar
a few drops of vanilla extract
a tiny pinch of salt
1 egg yolk
$1/4$ cup plain flour
2 tbsp chocolate chips

For the hot chocolate
$3/4$ mug milk
6 squares chocolate
a pinch of chilli powder

---

1. Put the butter in a large mug and microwave for 20 seconds until melted.
2. Stir in the sugars, vanilla and salt, then stir in the egg yolk followed by the flour and chocolate chips. Microwave for 40 seconds until cooked through.
3. Leave to stand while you make the hot chocolate.
4. Put the milk, chocolate and chilli in a second mug and microwave for 30 seconds.
5. Stir well, then continue to microwave in 20-second bursts, stirring between each burst, until the chocolate has melted, the milk is as hot as you like it and the ingredients are well blended.
6. Whisk well, then serve with the warm cookie.

MICROWAVE MERINGUES

Not as smooth as a traditional meringue but so quick and easy you'll wonder why you've never made meringues this way before. This makes more than one serving, of course, but since they keep well in an airtight container, it's worth using up a single egg white. Alternatively, it's an easy way to use up odd bits of egg white.

---

1 egg white, lightly beaten
2 cups icing sugar

---

1. Put a strip of baking paper in a large mug so that it goes down one side, across the bottom and up the other side.
2. Whisk the icing sugar into the egg white until you have a thick mixture. Using 2 spoons or your hands dusted in icing sugar, shape it into golf-ball-sized balls.
3. Put one ball in the mug and microwave for about 30 seconds until the meringue has puffed up and filled the mug. Use the paper to help you lift out the meringue, then repeat with the remaining meringue balls. This will make 10–12 meringues.

Index

120